John God[ber]

Plays: 3

Up 'n' Under, April in Paris, Perfect Pitch

Up 'n' Under: 'Hysterical one-liners and bawdy laddish rugby humour litter the dialogue' *The Stage*

Perfect Pitch: 'Godber's funny and cleverly turned piece. Takes what could be an episode from an edgy but cosy sitcom and makes of it something revealing. The play begins as a gentle parody of middle-class pretensions, a parody in which practical skills and sexual prowess are equated. It turns into a study of unkindness.' *Observer*

April in Paris: 'As for Godber he has arrived as playwright who can combine comedy, depth and feeling.' *Financial Times*

John Godber was born in Upton, near Pontefract, in 1956. He trained as a teacher at Bretton Hall College, Wakefield, did an MA in Drama and an MPhil/PhD in Drama at Leeds University. Since 1984 he has been Artistic Director of Hull Truck Theatre Company. His plays include: *Happy Jack*; *September in the Rain*; *Bouncers* (winner of seven Los Angeles Critics Circle awards); *Up 'n' Under* (Olivier Comedy of the Year Award, 1984); *Shakers* and *Shakers Restirred* (both with Jane Thornton); *Up 'n' Under 2*; *Blood, Sweat and Tears*; *Teechers*; *Salt of the Earth*; *On the Piste*; *Happy Families*; *The Office Party*; *April in Paris*; *Passion Killers* and *Lucky Sods*; *Perfect Pitch*; *Seasons in the Sun*; *Departures*; *Men of the World* and *Reunion*. Television and film work includes: *The Ritz*; *The Continental*; *My Kingdom for a Horse*; *Chalkface* (all BBC2), episodes of *Crown Court*; *Grange Hill* and *Brookside* and screenplays for *On the Piste* and *Up 'n' Under*. He is an honorary lecturer at Bretton Hall College and a D.Litt. of Hull and Lincoln Universities.

JOHN GODBER

Plays: 3

Up 'n' Under
April in Paris
Perfect Pitch

Foreword by the author
Introduced by John Bennett

Methuen Drama

METHUEN CONTEMPORARY DRAMATISTS

Published by Methuen 2003

1 3 5 7 9 10 8 6 4 2

First published in 2003 by
Methuen Publishing Limited
215 Vauxhall Bridge Road
London SW1V 1EJ

Introduction and collection copyright © John Godber 2003

Up 'n' Under first published in Great Britain in 1985 by Samuel French Ltd,
April in Paris first published in 1993 by Samuel French Ltd and
Perfect Pitch first published in 2002 by Samuel French Ltd.

John Godber has asserted his right under the Copyright, Designs
and Patents Act, 1988, to be identified as the author of this work.

Methuen Publishing Limited Reg. No. 3543167

A CIP catalogue record for this book is available from the British Library

ISBN 0 413 77304 3

Typeset by SX Composing DTP, Rayleigh, Essex
Printed and bound in Great Britain by
Cox & Wyman Ltd, Reading, Berkshire

Contents

A Chronology

1977   *Bouncers*, Edinburgh Festival; revived by Hull Truck Theatre Company at the Donmar Warehouse in 1984.

1981   *Cry Wolf*, Yorkshire Actors company

1981   *Cramp*, Edinburgh Festival; revived at Bloomsbury Theatre in 1987

1982   *EPA* (Minsthorpe High School)

1983   *Young Hearts Run Free* (Bretton Hall)

1984   *A Christmas Carol* (adaptation, Hull Truck)

1984   *September in the Rain* (Hull Truck)

1984   *Up 'n' Under 1* (Hull Truck, Edinburgh Festival; transferred to Donmar Warehouse)

1984   *Shakers* (with Jane Thornton, Hull Truck)

1985   *Happy Jack* (Hull Truck)

1985   *Up 'n' Under 2* (Hull Truck)

1986   *Cramp* (Musical. Hull Truck)

1986   *Blood, Sweat and Tears* (Hull Truck; then Tricycle Theatre)

1987   *Oliver Twist* (Hull Truck)

1987   *Teechers* (Hull Truck, Edinburgh Festival; revived at the Arts Theatre, 1988)

1988   *Salt of the Earth* (Wakefield Centenary; then Hull Truck, Edinburgh Festival; then Donmar Warehouse)

1989   *Office Party* (Nottingham Playhouse)

1990   *On the Piste* (Hull Truck, Derby Playhouse; then Garrick, 1993)

1991   *Everyday Heroes* (with Jane Thornton, Community Play, Bassetlaw)

1991   *Bouncers, 1990s Re-mix* (Hull Truck)

1991   *Shakers Re-stirred* (with Jane Thornton, Hull Truck)

1991   *Happy Families* (Little Theatre Guild, then West Yorkshire Playhouse, 1992)

1992   *April in Paris* (Hull Truck; then Ambassadors, 1994)

1994 *Passion Killers* (Hull Truck, Derby Playhouse)

1995 *Lucky Sods* (Hull Truck; then Hampstead Theatre)

1995 *Dracula* (with Jane Thornton, Hull Truck)

1996 *Gym and Tonic* (Hull Truck, Derby Playhouse)

1997 *Weekend Breaks* (Hull Truck, Alhambra, Bradford)

1997 *It Started with a Kiss* (Hull Truck)

1998 *Unleashed* (Hull Truck, Edinburgh Festival; then Bloomsbury, 1999)

1998 *Hooray for Hollywood* (Hull Truck)

1998 *Perfect Pitch* (Stephen Joseph Theatre, Scarborough)

1999 *Big Trouble in the Little Bedroom* (Hull Truck)

2000 *Seasons in the Sun* (Hull Truck, West Yorkshire Playhouse)

2000 *Thick as a Brick* (Hull Truck)

2001 *This House* (Hull Truck)

2001 *Departures* (Bolton Octagon Theatre, then Hull Truck)

2002 *Moby Dick* (with Nick Lane, Hull Truck)

2002 *Young Hearts* (co-production with Bransholme Kingswood Secondary School, Ferens Art Gallery, Hull Truck then Edinburgh Fringe Festival)

2002 *Men of the World* (Sheffield Crucible Theatre, then Hull Truck)

2002 *Reunion* (Hull Truck)

We gratefully acknowledge the help of John Bennett and Liverpool Hope University College in the preparation of this chronology. Further information can be found at *www.johngodber.co.uk*

Foreword

I am lucky as a writer to be able to direct my own plays, and extra lucky to have a theatre, Hull Truck, in which to put them on. It was never planned like this, events simply developed and I responded to them. Over time I have come to realise that every play has its own special mechanics and reasons for existing – these three plays are no exception.

This collection serves as an example of three distinct styles of theatre, each with its own language and rules, brought about under distinct, unique conditions. It also illustrates my development as a writer after leaving teaching in 1983.

I joined Hull Truck Theatre Company as Artistic Director in January 1984. At the first board meeting I was informed that the company was insolvent and that drastic measures had to be put in place in order for it to survive. Box office figures were dreadful, and the good people of Hull were staying away from what was then Spring Street Theatre in their droves. Interestingly enough none of this was mentioned at my interview.

I had never run a Theatre Company before, but as a drama teacher at Minsthorpe High School, a West Yorkshire comprehensive, I had fantasised about the type of work I would programme if I was ever lucky enough to be elevated to run Leeds Playhouse. For a start the opening season would feature a collection of German Expressionist plays; popularism was out of the question. Having been influenced by the German Theatre expert Dr Mike Patterson whilst studying part-time for a Ph.D., at Leeds University I had dreamed of directing Kaiser, Büchner and Brecht. However the cold reality of running a theatre in Hull in 1984, convinced me to body swerve the expressionists and look at themes a little more local.

It was patently clear from that first board meeting that the company needed plays that would put 'bums on seats'. With this in mind I took myself up to Whitley Bay with the intention of writing a play about Rugby League. *Up 'n' Under* was sketched out in less than a week; a simple enough story, a kind of triumph in the face of adversity. With a limited budget – something that I had lived with as a teacher – I set out to make a piece of popular theatre that would attract the largely non-theatre-going public in Hull. I would use cod-Shakespearean verse, dream sequences, slow motions action, reverse action, direct audience address, voice over. Whatever is at the playwright's disposal I used in writing *Up 'n' Under*.

*

I have written extensively about my interest in physical theatre in the introduction to Godber Plays: 1, so I will avoid repetition here. Suffice to say that writing a play about rugby gave me the opportunity to experiment with physical theatre once more. A third of the play is an actual game of rugby, so we had to be inventive. As a writer I had to direct the play in my head as I worked out the physical moves.

We opened the play at the Edinburgh Festival in 1984 with the audience cheering every try; the play won the Olivier Award for Best Comedy in 1984 and played in the West End for almost two years making various return visits during the mid-nineties. As far as audiences in Hull were concerned they were happy to watch a play which reflected aspects of their social life. I would love to say that in one 'foul swoop' we had turned the theatre's fortunes around – almost but not quite. What was fascinating during the *Up 'n' Under* years was that whilst the game of rugby on stage was nothing short of a dance, not one of the professional rugby players who saw it said it was anything other than realistic. It became clear to me that things can be emotionally real without descending into superficial realism.

So is *Up 'n' Under* a great play on the page? Well, in all honesty, probably not. Is it an exciting evening in the theatre, and is it a good example of physical theatre communicating itself directly and evocatively to an audience? Unquestionably yes, and whilst there have been pale replicas, on its day, to use sporting parlance, there is very little to touch it.

*

April in Paris is a two-hander which tells the story of Al and Bet as they break out of their humdrum life in Hull and discover Paris for the first time. The play was commissioned for the Hull Festival in 1992, and had the same job as *Up 'n' Under*, to put 'bums on seats'. A number of metropolitan critics took exception to Al and Bet's journey, contesting that no one of their age had not been to Paris in the 1990s, and that their conversion to becoming art-lovers was too easy. Now, of course, I would disagree, that's obvious, but few observers actually picked up on the heightened sense of language in the play and the poetic way in which Al and Bet communicate. This language kicks the play away from reality and places the characters in a parallel theatrical world. We recognise the world we are watching, but it's a long way from Zola. I suppose I mustn't be too upset by critics, after all, we are all critics.

The first act of *April in Paris* takes place on a ten-foot piece of white plastic, this serves as Al and Bet's home, and the ferry in which they cross the North Sea. Whilst writing the play I worked with designer Rob Jones just to see how little we would need to make the transformations from one location to the other. Again, it was important for me to allow the play to be theatrical. By choosing to write a play about a trip to Paris we had to take the audience on the voyage with us. Of course most of the voyage was in the imagination of the audience. There are clearly compromises whenever you start writing, the limits of one's imagination for a start, that's a fairly big one, the other major one in my experience has been money. Two actors in a play may be a producer's dream, but it certainly raises huge questions for the writer.

Should these two actors only play themselves, should they speak to the audience, should they play other characters? As with *Up 'n' Under* I was able to draw on a variety of theatrical techniques in order to allow two actors to tell their story, and get us out of the 'room'. *April in Paris* certainly uses direct audience address, but the physical aspects of the show are much less rigorous than the earlier play. The Paris that Al and Bet experience is described from their point of view, and the graphic image is created in the mind of the viewer, there is much less sweat here.

Whilst *April in Paris* is distinctly less energetic, it does boast a development in style within the work. The play starts with Al and Bet grunting at each other. These grunts are a kind of poetry – the couple have worn together like two stones, constantly bickering and argumentative. They speak, but they do not listen. They exist with each other but have forgotten how to care. However as they begin their journey they are given to express themselves with more panache and detail. When they eventually board the boat they speak directly to the audience, and indeed they describe how they feel about Paris, before returning to their grunting existence on return home. They have come full circle, but the paradox is clear, the more you know, the more you know you don't know.

Theatre need not be a 'slice of life viewed through a temperament'. Within certain conditions anything can happen as long as the rules are laid out clearly from the start, and then even those rules can change at times.

*

Perfect Pitch, written some six years after *April in Paris*, and commissioned by the Stephen Joseph Theatre Scarborough, is a different proposition altogether. This was the first time I had written specifically for a space that was in-the-round. However, the onus to fill the theatre was just the same, as were the cast limitations.

Scarborough threw up a new challenge, and one which I didn't fully appreciate straight away. I mentioned that in the previous two plays the characters spoke directly to the audience to evoke various places and feelings. However, when working in-the-round this was less easy to do since if you addressed the audience you would have your back to the other three sides. Consequently *Perfect Pitch* was a first for me; essentially a piece of fly-on-the-wall realism.

My plays start out as films in my head – then I have to use all the skills at my disposal to turn them into theatrical events. Being unable to address the audience directly, as I

had done in *Up 'n' Under* and *April in Paris*, *Perfect Pitch*
presented me with a range of problems, problems which the
dramatists of the 'well-made play' had wrestled with a
hundred years earlier. I had to write a play which took place
in a single location. How dull, I thought!

Since I had set *Perfect Pitch* on a caravan site on the
Scarborough coast, I began to wonder how I could add my
innate sense of theatricality to this jejune location. Should
the play be set in real time, would that work, was there a
way of cutting through time, fast-forwarding so that I could
get a sense of pace to the piece? Clearly the thought of being
in one space for two hours worried me. I had often said in
interviews that I didn't want to leave my room at home to
sit in someone else's room in the theatre for two hours. In
the end I decided to introduce the play with a number of so-
called 'stills'. Short scenes which might consist of a line or
two but which gave a sense of atmosphere and allowed time
to pass. This created – in my head at least – a filmic sense of
pace.

This restriction on the so-called 'style' of the play
frustrated me at first since I was writing a play which
'anyone' could write. A bog-standard piece of fourth wall
realism in essence. My previous work including the plays
listed above had always rallied against the confines of the
fourth wall. They were flamboyantly anti-naturalistic, they
looked for theatrical style where ever they could, and often,
even by my own admission at the expense of the content.
Their form searched tirelessly for the theatrical excitement
that had first plugged me into theatre as a live and special
event quite distinct from television.

I mentioned at the beginning of this ramble, that this
collection demonstrates something of an arc in my
development. That is not to say that I consider my
graduation to fourth-wall realism as unquestionably a good
thing. Whilst *Perfect Pitch* is widely regarded as a 'good play',
it doesn't have any of the verve or theatrical panache that
Up 'n' Under enjoys. But then again its characters are
grounded and three-dimensional, and that case cannot be
put for *Up 'n' Under*, and I have to admit to myself that it is

more carefully written – perhaps experience is a defining factor here?

What has become clear to me over time, is that quite often the play and the subject matter picks the style. Looking back it would have been impossible to make *Up 'n' Under* into a well-made play and still play a game of rugby on stage. In any case David Storey had done that twenty years earlier with *The Changing Room*, and since I had written an MA Thesis on David Storey I was keen not to re-plough that territory.

Scholars will no doubt recognise a number of recurring themes in these three plays; all three concern themselves with leisure activities, they are not work plays. It is probably fair to say that the characters are from working-class backgrounds, and that redundancy plays a major part in all their lives. Whilst they may change in style there is also a sense of humour and a dryness of wit which is I suppose very much in a gritty Yorkshire tradition.

It is fascinating to fleetingly apply oneself to consider the nature of one's work. When working in a producing theatre, lack of time and the meeting of deadlines often precludes such analysis. I suppose in a way there is always a constant repositioning of what makes good theatre and what makes a good play. A strong literary tradition is often cited as the backbone for a good play, but we have all witnessed 'good plays' die, and equally, the effusive energy of physical comedy has been known to have its off days. What keeps theatre a source of inspiration and frustration is the plethora of potential styles at a writer's disposal. For me, the way he or she tells a story is just as important as the story itself – form and content co-exist but can often counter-point. Whatever the relationship between form and content, and whatever style a writer might settle on, we have to acknowledge that theatre remains an organic and ever-shifting target, and as some one who has worked in it for twenty years that's both reassuring and unsettling.

John Godber
Hull 2003

Introduction

The plays in this collection, *Up 'n' Under*, *April in Paris*, *Perfect Pitch*, demonstrate the range of a playwright primarily associated in the minds of the theatre-going public with his earliest play, the youth-oriented, 'in-yer-face' physicality of the four male, multi-character performers in *Bouncers*. These three later plays provide a useful taxonomy for the extensive and wide-ranging Godber canon; a range that includes the physical (*Up 'n' Under*), but also encompasses the ritualised biographical (*April in Paris*) and the later, more naturalistic, class-conflict based work (*Perfect Pitch*).

The three plays share a genesis of a specifically northern commission by, respectively, Hull Truck Theatre, the Hull Literary Festival and the Stephen Joseph Theatre in Scarborough. They were each initially written for a particular audience but have gone on to demonstrate national and even international resonance; *April in Paris*, for example, has been staged in New York, Israel, Denmark and, naturally enough, Paris.

The plays are markedly different in form, ranging from the cartoon-like dynamism of *Up 'n' Under* to the naturalistic credibility of *Perfect Pitch* via the stylised economy of *April in Paris*. However, despite the different initial audiences and differing performance styles there are common themes underpinning all three: active women coping with passive men, domestic relationships and friendships under strain and the potential transformative power of leisure. This latter element of transformation will be discussed in greater detail in relation to each of the plays. They also share a mission to entertain – to attract and retain an audience that may be more 'at home', literally and metaphorically, with a televisual and cinematic culture than with the 'willing suspension of disbelief' which characterises the performative contract of fourth-wall naturalism.

Above all else, they are significant examples of popular theatre – a theatre accessible to an audience sometimes ignored by mainstream performance values, an audience for whom the choice of leisure activity is not so much a question of where but who, not where to holiday but who am I? Many in Godber's popular theatre audience can identify with characters exercised by how they choose to spend their usually all-too-brief or otherwise enforced and lengthy leisure.

- I might be a butcher by occupation but I'm also a Rugby League player
- I might have a mindless job but I can still exercise my mind by entering competitions
- I might be part of what some perceive as the unemployed under-class but I'm a first-class breeder of bull terriers
- I might have a job that requires little imagination but I can choose to spend the occasional evening in the imaginative world of live theatre

These are frequently the parameters of Godber's characters' lives. The plays, written during the middle-to-late period of Margaret Thatcher's administration, consciously construct leisure, rather than work, as the determining factor in positive self-definition.

*

A popular leisure activity and one that contributes more than a little to a positive sense of self, particularly in Godber's native Yorkshire, is the playing or watching of Rugby League. It is important to note a significant regional distinction here, as the professional game of Rugby League is primarily seen as province of the northern working man and woman, whereas the once-amateur game of Rugby Union is traditionally associated with the south of the country. Godber has experience of both games, having played union at university and watched league games to assist the writing of *Up 'n' Under* and to research one of the passions of his Hull audience.

It is difficult to gain a true sense of the theatrical impact of *Up 'n' Under* from reading the text. The piece is not so much a play as an event, drawing its audience into the heat of the game and encouraging vocal support for the

struggling Wheatsheaf team. Successful productions have
the audience leaping from their seats, cheering the training
and the tries and sighing with partisan fervour as the final
kick misses its mark. This vocal and emotive audience
participation provides a useful key to a reading of the play
as a particular kind of popular theatre – melodrama. Reg is
clearly the villain, corrupt, manipulative and keen to exploit
the naivety of Arthur and the team who become combined
de facto heroine, out of their depth and in dire need of rescue.
Enter Hazel, our trans-gendered hero, who not only
transforms the team in a matter of weeks but joins them in
the David vs. Goliath struggle of the climactic match. There
is a consistent use of music to underscore emotive moments
in the play (melodrama translates as 'music drama') from
the use of the evocative *Rocky* theme to the team's choric
singing of an earthier version of Billy Bennett's 1920s music-
hall staple, *She Was Poor But She Was Honest.*

This passionate audience engagement is due to the
quality of Godber's stagecraft. Critics dismiss Frank and
Hazel's blank verse parodic chorus speeches as owing too
much to early Steven Berkoff plays such as *East* but they fail
to appreciate Godber's knowing, irreverent, post-modern
juxtaposition of high and low-culture, of William
Shakespeare and Sylvester Stallone – *Henry V* meets *Rocky I.*
Another crucial element of this stagecraft is the intense
physicality of the play, the 'sweat' as Godber calls it. This is
vital to the enjoyment of the last scene in Act One and
drives the genuine tension of the final match. These scenes'
playful intertextual referencing of the *Rocky* theme music
and ideals lift spirits onstage and in the auditorium.

The most significant moment of theatrical invention is the
staging of the match itself. Rather like Anthony Shaffer's
1970 thriller, *Sleuth*, original programmes for *Up 'n' Under*
suggest a cast larger than actually appears onstage in order
to not, appropriately enough, give the game away. The
moment when the actors, in their double-sided kit, run
down-stage and spin through one hundred and eighty
degrees to reveal their Cobblers Arms identity to the
audience never fails to produce a cheer and spontaneous

applause in any decently-staged production; it is a genuine *coup-de-théâtre*. The match itself is a joyous mix of real-time, slow motion and fast forward action, allowing the audience's expertise as sports fans a rare moment of high-culture legitimacy or, as Alastair Macauley described the play in the *Financial Times* in 1995, 'they come knowing all about rugby, and they leave learning much about theatre'.[1]

In *Up 'n' Under*, Godber has created a contemporary melodrama without the traditional ending of last-moment rescue. The hero, Hazel, manages to transform the fortunes of the team to the point where they have a chance of victory but the 'heroine' Arthur misses the vital kick. This is a consciously incomplete transformation and lends the play more credibility than a simple happy ending ever could. I would suggest that it is its very lack of well-made play credentials; its fast-paced, two-dimensional, cartoon-like quality that makes it a rare play, a popular contemporary melodrama that engages its audience in a truly theatrical event. Some of the dialogue may be overly economic at times and the characters may not stand detailed Chekhovian analysis of their motivation but I have yet to see an audience stamp and cheer in recognition of the exquisitely crafted moment of the shooting in *Uncle Vanya* in the way they support the expertly choreographed, match-turning half-time try of Arthur Hoyle. As Godber, citing the pioneering theatre designer and critic Edward Gordon Craig, states in his programme notes to the original production of *Up 'n' Under*, 'it is the dancer and not the poet who is father to the theatre'.[2]

*

After achieving a coveted Fringe First at the Edinburgh Festival in 1984 and winning the Society of West End Theatres award for best comedy in the same year, *Up 'n' Under* enjoyed a long run at the Fortune Theatre in London's West End. The plays of John Godber do not always enjoy such metropolitan success; London audiences, proud of their sophistication in so many respects, seem to struggle to accept the specific regional nuances of dialect and general 'Yorkshireness' of some of the later Godber works. *April in Paris* played at the Ambassadors Theatre in London for fifteen weeks in 1992. There was an unusually famous cast: the late Gary Olsonn as Al and the singer Maria Friedman as Bet. Reviews were mixed but Malcolm Rutherford described Godber, as 'one of the best contemporary British playwrights'.[3]

However, some critics accused Godber of an 'unearned optimism' in the play, considering the transformation of Al from morose, monochrome malcontent into sprightly, technicolour optimist to be, rather as the five-week transformation of the Wheatsheaf Arms from no-hopers to giant-killers, insufficiently justified by the text. What they failed to appreciate was the frustrated artistic potential of Al. Frustration is a common theme in Godber's more biographical work, the frustration of a man – sometimes a woman as in *Blood, Sweat and Tears* – with a desire to express him or herself but not the means, knowing that there must be more to living than existing but unsure how to access something more fulfilling. They also missed the poetry of the phatic dialogue that forms much of the first half of the play, the Pinteresque conversations where little is said but much is meant and even more is misunderstood. The short, non-verbal sounds, the 'ee's' and 'ah's' do not carry the same resonance for a southern ear as for a northern:

> What they'd missed was the nuance. What they couldn't get was the: Alreet? Alreet! To them that was just – all right! To a northern audience, it's music, it's poetry: How you feeling then? Not bad! That to me, that is an orchestra.[4]

The full subtlety of the play would have been available to anyone seeing the premiere at Hull Truck's Spring Street Theatre as Godber himself played Al and his partner, the playwright and actress Jane Thornton, played Bet. Godber, for reasons of economy as much as anything else, has appeared in many of his early biographical plays such as *Happy Jack*, *September in the Rain* and *Cramp*. *April in Paris* was to be his last venture on to the stage, apart from occasional unplanned performances when he has been forced on as an unlikely understudy due to cast illness.[5] This is a shame as, by many accounts and reviews, Godber the actor is every bit as theatrically effective as Godber the writer and director. It certainly meant that in this original production, there was very little that was missed in the way of the non-verbal tics and gestures that can be the hallmark of a marriage spent almost exclusively in each other's company.

It is worth noting that Godber directs the premieres of all his own plays and manages to elicit rounded performances and a wider emotional range than subsequent directors who, in general, have a tendency to go for the broad comic moments at the expense of the understated integrity of the characterisation. In his direction, Godber always manages to maintain a balance between the strident comedy of desperation and the quieter pathos of frustrated, unfulfilled lives. That is not to say that *April in Paris* is a genteel study of a relationship in decline, far from it. Lines such as 'Every time you get a bath there's a line of scum left around the bath. It's like your skin's peeling off. I have to get a cloth and scrape it off' are funny yet brutal testaments to a relationship failing due to the forced intimacy of people who would ordinarily spend much of their time at work and apart from each other.

The inventive stagecraft seen in *Up 'n' Under* is again employed here with the two actors conveying the cramped Paris Metro, the height of the Eiffel Tower or the unsteadiness of the ferry crossing purely through body posture and carefully choreographed rhythms. Godber's keen visual sense of theatre is also evidenced in the play through the simple use of a swinging light-fitting to suggest movement, or the placing of a life-belt to denote a change of scene from the interior of a room to the exterior of a ship or, the transformation of the minimal white walls of the Act One setting into the sumptuous, multi-coloured spectacle of a detail from Pierre Auguste Renoir's 1881 painting, *The Luncheon of the Boating Party*. If the plot of *Up 'n' Under* owes something to the *Rocky* films, then the design and narrative tone of *April in Paris* is indebted to *The Wizard of Oz*.

Popular theatre techniques are also evident; the local references as they sail from Hull, the direct address, and the emphasis on the virtuoso actor creating a performance without recourse to elaborate make-up or staging. As an aside, it is interesting to note that Al's comment on the transvestite Parisian cabaret at Madam Arthur's, 'I'd never thought I'd sit through owt like that, but I'll tell you this, they worked bloody hard', resonates with a comment from John McGrath's seminal work on popular theatre, *A Good Night Out: Popular Theatre, Audience, Class and Form*, where he talks of a working-class audience appreciating *effort* in performance; 'They like clear, worked-for results . . . They know it comes from skill and hard work, and they expect hard work and skill'.[6] *April in Paris* forms part of what has been described as Godber's 'Britons Abroad' trilogy, which includes the later Club 18–30 inspired play *Passion Killers* and the more famous skiing comedy *On the Piste*. All deal with the fish-out-of-water experience of the unsophisticated English traveller and the strain placed on already creaking relationships by the temporary licence to be somebody as 'different' as the exotic locations these couples holiday in.

*

The most recent play in this collection, *Perfect Pitch*, was a commission for Alan Ayckbourn's theatre in Scarborough. This is an interesting relationship as Godber and Ayckbourn are increasingly bracketed together by critics as champions of, respectively, a particular brand of accessible mainstream and popular comic theatre: Ayckbourn is the only living playwright in the country whose work is performed more often than John Godber's. *Perfect Pitch* differs from the other two plays in this collection in that it is entirely naturalistic; there is no direct address to the audience, no multi-character acting and no stylised stage setting. It is played in compressed real-time with no fast-forward or slow motion moments. There is a physicality of action of sorts in the play but the sexual gymnastics of Grant and Steph occur offstage and are suggested by sound. The play is an observational comedy of class differences with the middle-class regimented lives of Ron and Yvonne brought into sharp relief by the

free-wheeling indulgences of their working-class neighbours
– readers with knowledge of the Nietzschean approach to
the Greek classics will recognise an Apollonian versus a
Dionysian code. In this first professional liaison between
Ayckbourn and Godber, the playwright has skilfully
managed to satisfy both Scarborough and Hull audiences by
taking characters who would be at home in an Ayckbourn
play, Ron and Yvonne, and juxtaposing them with
characters more likely to be found in one of Godber's plays
– it is not difficult to think of Grant as one of the eponymous
Bouncers or Steph trapped in the monotony of a waitressing
job in *Shakers*.

Apart from notable exceptions such as *Up 'n' Under II* and
September in the Rain, Godber does not write sequels, the plays
tend to spring from immediate or recalled biographical
incident or a particular anxiety over an element of the
Zeitgeist. However, in this case it is possible to trace a
reasonably direct link with an earlier play, *Gym and Tonic*:
here the central character, Don, sees the solution to his mid-
life crisis as being the purchase of a caravan 'and an awning
for a barbecue.' The awning is one of the key metaphors in
Perfect Pitch for the declining relationship between Ron and
Yvonne. Godber clearly intends his audience to draw a
parallel between Ron's difficulties in erecting the awning
and another type of erection problem. The passionate, vocal
love-making so apparent from their neighbours serves only
to underscore this dysfunction and it gradually becomes
clear that Grant and Steph are leading more fulfilled, more
passionate lives than the supposedly culturally superior but
rather cold couple next door.

The pivotal scene in the play occurs when Steph
persuades Yvonne to see the male strippers in the local
theatre. Having religiously abstained from alcohol whilst
training, on this particular 'good night out', Yvonne
succumbs to temptation on every level. In a characteristic
piece of Godber stagecraft, the audience is presented with a
double focus, the sight of Steph and Yvonne appreciating
the physical prowess of the unseen male strippers as they, in
actuality, gaze upon the distinctly paunchy Ron as he

undresses for bed. The repetitive, nightly ritual that Yvonne must have witnessed for many years is neatly juxtaposed with the singularity of the special event that, whilst initially reluctant, Yvonne enjoys with a vigour that one suspects is never shared with Ron in their more intimate moments. It is surprising to note that later, non-Godber directed productions, actually have 'real' strippers on stage, which, apart from being prurient, dilutes one of the most powerful images in the play.

Matters reach their most brutal when Ron challenges Yvonne over the details of what happened during the night out and Yvonne, incensed by Ron's apathy and reserve, describes how the night with Steph and the strippers was 'the first time I've felt any excitement'; at this point, Ron slaps her across the face. It is a genuinely shocking moment and usually elicits gasps of disbelief from the audience. We have been led to believe that Grant and Steph are the brutal Neanderthals – at one point Steph has a black eye that is either the result of over-enthusiastic sexual activity or domestic violence (Godber intriguingly leaves this for the audience to decide), but there is no such equivocation in the attack on Yvonne, who then fights back, and husband and wife 'wrestle awkwardly'. Grant enters, we assume, disturbed by the noises coming from Ron and Yvonne's caravan. The semi-articulate villain of the first half now appears as pot-bellied hero, reminding Ron that 'tha's not at school now!' and lecturing him on violence against women. It is an effective and entirely credible role-reversal and gives the play an unexpected yet satisfying edge.

Reviews of *Perfect Pitch* were very positive; one critic described it as 'Godber's funniest and most acutely observed play'.[7] Ron hopes that the purchase of a new caravan will also buy them a new lifestyle and possibly new lives; yet Godber makes it clear that they bring their old lives with them, the light classical music, the David Lodge novel, the imagery of the preserved Betaware containers all suggest a transportation of a lifestyle, rather than a transformation. It is Yvonne who travels the furthest distance metaphorically, her evening with Steph transforms her into a more elemental creature, someone capable of living in and being of the moment rather than the more traditional, middle-class, deferred-gratification existence she has lead so far. The whole situation is beautifully underscored by Ron finally finding the elusive assembly instructions for the awning, suggesting that he may have also discovered his libido (or at least the instructions for it) but this is too little too late; Yvonne is listening to the sounds of Grant and Steph's passionate love-making at the end of the play.

These three plays show something of the range of one of this country's most popular playwrights. They demonstrate differing experiments in form, physical theatre, minimalist storytelling, naturalism; and an unerring instinct in matching this form to a variety of content. *Up 'n' Under*, *April in Paris* and *Perfect Pitch* are good examples of Godber's particular brand of popular theatre, where he debates frustration and transformation, the nature of leisure as empowerment but also as artistic, social or sexual impotence. A final link, which, I hope this introduction has made clear, is the proactive nature of the female characters in all three plays, Hazel, Bet and Yvonne all pursue an activity they enjoy, whether it is physical training or the mental exercise of entering competitions, they do something for themselves rather than, as their male partners, complain about what is, or has been done to them. For a writer sometimes accused of creating exclusively male-centred work, these plays have a surprisingly feminist streak to them.

John Bennett
Liverpool
April 2003

References

1 Alastair Macaulay, 'A Playwright Scores Sweetly', *Financial Times*, 11 March 1995.
2 Edward Gordon Craig, *On the Art of the Theatre*, Theatre Arts Books, New York, 1982.
3 Malcolm Rutherford, 'April in Paris', *Financial Times*, 3 February 1992.

4 John Godber in conversation with Jude Kelly at the West Yorkshire Playhouse, 21 November 1995. Full transcript available from the John Godber website, www.johngodber.co.uk.

5 Hull Truck Theatre usually does not provide understudies and John Godber has had to read in for indisposed cast members on various occasions; he once appeared as a stand-in for an actress playing a 15-year-old female pupil in his 1999 musical, *Thick as a Brick*.

6 John McGrath, *A Good Night Out: Popular Theatre, Audience, Class and Form*, Methuen, 1981.

7 Lyn Gardner, 'Perfect Pitch', *The Guardian*, 21 October 1999.

Up 'n' Under

To the Rugby League fans of Hull

Up 'n' Under premiered at the Assembly Rooms of the
Edinburgh Festival in August 1984. The cast was as follows:

Arthur	Peter Geeves
Frank	Richard Ridings
Steve/Reg	Andrew Dunn
Tony	Chris Walker
Hazel	June Clifford
Phil	Richard May

Directed by John Godber
Sound designed by Alan McDevitt
Music by Steve Pinnock

Act One

Frank, **Hazel**, **Tony** *and* **Phil** *enter. They stand along the back.*
Frank *takes a rugby shirt from the hooks and passes it across to*
Hazel. *She catches it and places it carefully over the sit-ups rack.*
Frank *takes up the speech.*

Frank   Here on the very playing fields of Castleford your
eyes will gaze in awe at splendid sights unseen . . . Your
mind will jump and question the wisdom of our tale . . . But
we care not. So, let battle cries be heard across our fair isle,
from Hull . . . to Liverpool. Let trumpets sound and brass
bands play their Hovis tunes.

Hazel *throws the ball (which she has by now picked up from the
bench) to* **Frank**, *then retreats back to her position.*

For here, upon this very stage, we see amateur Rugby
League, a game born of rebellion, born of divide in eighteen
ninety-five. For the working class of the North, for the
working class. All around, pub teams throng the bars, club
teams meet in lowly courts, amateurs all. Yet even as I speak
a game commences in this battling competition; the
Crooked Billet from Rochdale, play the Cobblers Arms
from Castleford: unbeaten gods of amateur Rugby sevens,
unbeaten many seasons with greatness thrust upon them.
Yet many know this to be true, still, one man takes the stage
– our hero: Arthur Hoyle, a very lowly figure, yet the stature
of a lion, a painter and decorator by trade. His quest will be
within our two-hour traffic, to challenge the might of the
Cobblers, to throw down the gauntlet and hope to break the
myth that is the Cobblers Arms . . . His journey may be long
and weary, and though you must travel with him, you never
can assist, no matter how you pine to; your role is but to sit,
and watch. Yet soft, for as you gaze upon our breezeblock
'O' Reg Welsh appears, manager of the Cobblers, and
trainer of their team; a very big fish on this our dish of
amateur Rugby League. Here before your very eyes, two
rivals meet: Reg and Arth.

Reg *and* **Arthur** *enter.*

Reg   Arthur.

Arthur   Reg.

Frank   And they will bet in lofty sums. But mark this, Arthur's coffers are very low, his mouth is very loose, and oft this and his brain are as separate as two mighty continents. My masters, is he mad or what is he? He is apt to make daft bets . . . to idle threats and boasts. From me enough, I let them play their stuff. So let our story now unfold, as two great rivals pledge their gold . . .

Reg   Arthur.

Arthur   Reg . . .

Reg   How are you, sunshine?

Arthur   Not bad . . .

Reg   How's the wife?

Arthur   Still living in the same house.

Reg   Like that, is it, Arthur?

Arthur   You know Doreen, Reg, she'd argue with fog.

Reg   Takes after you, Arthur.

Arthur   Dunno.

Reg   No.

Arthur   No, I've changed, Reg . . . I was a hot-head, you know that as well as anybody . . . I've cooled down.

Reg   Good to hear that, Arth.

Arthur   Well, old age and poverty helps, doesn't it?

Reg   Dunno about the poverty.

Arthur   No, right.

Reg   You did some daft things in your day, Arthur lad.

Arthur I know.

Reg Can you remember when you poked the linesman in the eye at Warrington?

Arthur I can . . .

Reg And when you head-butted the referee at St Helens?

Arthur Yeah.

Reg Eh, and when you burnt down the goal posts at 'unslett?

Arthur Oh, for disagreeing with that offside decision.

Reg Didn't see that one, read about it in the paper.

Arthur Good times, Reg.

Reg Yes.

Arthur Good times.

Reg I must say, Arthur . . . it's good to see you settled.

Arthur Oh yeah . . .

Reg The way you were going I never thought you'd make thirty . . .

Arthur No . . .

Reg You could still have been playing.

Arthur If it hadn't been for you, Reg . . .

Reg Now don't be like that, Arth.

Arthur But it's true, you were on the board that got me banned, you know that as much as anybody.

Reg Let's not get in to all that . . .

Arthur You brought it up.

Reg No matter what I say to you I'll not convince you that it wasn't only me who pushed to have you banned . . . no matter what I say . . .

Arthur   That's the way I saw it, anyway . . .

A beat.

Reg   Cigar?

Arthur   Don't smoke.

Reg   Still fit . . . ?

Arthur   Still trying . . .

Reg   Good to hear it.

Arthur   We can't all live a life of leisure, can we Reg?

Reg   But I've worked for it, Arthur sunshine . . . worked for it . . . making money is all about having money, investing money.

Arthur   Yeah . . .

Reg   You must have a bob or two?

Arthur   I've got a bob or two.

Reg   I thought so . . .

Arthur   And that's all I've got.

Reg   What do you think to my lads this year?

Arthur   All right.

Reg   Come on, Arthur . . . they're more than all right, they're magnificent . . . The Magnificent Seven, that's what I call them.

Arthur   They've got their problems, Reg.

Reg   What do you mean?

Arthur   They're good on the ball . . .

Reg   Yeah . . .

Arthur   Bad in defence.

Reg   Give over . . . their defence is clam-tight . . .

Arthur   No, is it heck . . .

Reg   It is.

Arthur   Well, you take it from me.

Reg   The Cobblers'll beat any side you want to name.

Arthur   They're not that good, Reg . . . listen to me, I'm telling you.

Reg   I thought you might have learnt some sense as times go on . . . pity you haven't . . . same old Arthur.

Arthur   Same old Reg . . . full of shit.

Reg   Oh, you're not worth talking to.

Arthur   The truth hurts.

Reg   You make me laugh . . . a feller with half an eye could see how good they are.

Arthur   In that case I must be going blind.

Reg   Look at that . . . free and economic distribution . . . fast hands . . . unbeatable . . . completely unbeatable.

Arthur   No.

Reg   They are.

Arthur   Reg, they're not . . .

Reg   I'm not arguing with you . . . you know I'm right.

Arthur   I could train a team to beat 'em.

Reg   Talk sense.

Arthur   I'm talking sense.

Reg   Doesn't sound much sense to me . . .

Arthur   I could get a team together to beat the Cobblers.

Reg   Have you had some beer?

Arthur   No . . .

Reg   Can you hear what you're saying?

Arthur   I know what I'm saying and I mean it . . . I've thought it for years.

Reg   Arthur, you're talking out of your arsehole.

Arthur   Steady.

Reg   You are talking utter crap and you know it.

Arthur   No, I'm not. I could get a team to beat 'em.

Reg   Don't be such a pillock.

Arthur   I said steady with the language, Reg.

Reg   Well, you're talking such rubbish, man.

Arthur   I'm not talking rubbish, I'm talking facts . . . there's a way to beat these, no problem.

Reg   There's no way you're gonna get an amateur club to beat these, no way.

Arthur   Rubbish.

Reg   No way.

Arthur   Rubbish.

Reg   No way, Arthur . . .

Arthur   I could do it . . . I could train any team in the North to beat these.

Reg   Okay then, put your money where your mouth is.

Arthur   Eh . . . ?

Reg   Put your money where your mouth is . . .

Arthur   Ar . . . dunno . . .

Reg   See what I mean . . . You're the one who's full of shit.

Arthur   All right, then, I bet you . . .

Reg   That you can train a given team to beat my lads?

Arthur   Yeah, I bet you, Reg.

Reg   How much? Four grand . . . five thousand . . . ten thousand, Arthur? Let's make it a decent bet, shall we?

Arthur   I bet my mortgage . . .

Reg   What about Doreen?

Arthur   I bet my house . . .

Reg   Keep it sensible . . .

Arthur   I bet my house that I can get a team to beat them set of nancy poofters, Reg Welsh . . . that's the bet, shake on it . . .

Reg   You'll lose . . .

Arthur   We'll see . . .

Reg   I mean it.

Arthur   Any team in the North, come on, name a club side . . . I'll train 'em.

Reg   We'll meet in the next sevens.

Arthur   When is it?

Reg   Five weeks' time . . .

Arthur   That's great . . . name my name.

Reg   No turning back . . .

Arthur   You've got my word . . .

Reg   It's a bet?

Arthur   Come on, name the team I've got to train.

Reg   I'll make arrangements for us to meet in the draw.

Arthur   I'll leave the dirty work to you.

Reg   I'll pull a few influential strings.

Arthur   What's the team, Reg . . . ?

Reg   I name the Wheatsheaf from near Hull.

Arthur   Nice one . . . now name a team.

Reg   I name the Wheatsheaf, Arthur.

Arthur   The *Wheatsheaf Arms*?

Reg   That's the one.

Arthur   You're joking.

Reg   The bet's on . . .

Arthur   Bloody hell . . .

Reg   Five weeks then, Arthur . . . I look forward to the game . . .

Reg *exits.*

Arthur   The *Wheatsheaf*?

Arthur *exits.*

Hazel   Now, hear this news of the Wheatsheaf . . . The Wheatsheaf pub . . . infamous in rugby circles. Yet in all their history they have never won a single game, and what's the same, they never have seven men. As you saw, Arthur's head was loose, he wished he'd shut his gob. You know right well the bet is unfair, but to pull out now would be disaster. The path he treads is narrow and long . . . the job is on . . . to train this team into the likes of which has ne'er been seen.

Hazel *exits.*

The lights come up on **Frank**, **Tony** *and* **Phil**, *who are sitting despondently in their dressing-room.*

Frank   Give 'em another five minutes . . . then . . . home . . .

Phil   There is a brighter side to it, historically speaking.

Tony   What?

Phil   The long-running tradition of the Wheatsheaf team losing, because of lack of players.

Tony   I wonder what's happened to Steve and Tommy?

Frank   Steve'll be messing about with his car putting new headlights on it . . . or cleaning the engine down with Palmolive.

Tony   It's a smart car he's got . . . goes like a bomb.

Frank   It ought to go like a bomb and blow his bloody head off.

Phil   Sick jokes . . .

Frank   Thank you, doctor.

Tony   Well, anyway, this is my last game.

Phil   And me . . . the last time I'm going to look a prat.

Tony   If we can't get seven then that's it for me, anyway, you don't look a prat.

Phil *notices* **Tony** *has no socks.*

Phil   Where's your socks?

Tony   Forgotten 'em.

Phil   Brilliant!

Tony   I can't afford to be going out and buying sock after sock . . .

Phil   That's brilliant, that is, there's only three of us, and you two look pathetic. You could at least make an effort.

Frank   We have made an effort, we've turned up.

Phil   You're not playing in them, are you?

Frank   What?

Phil   Jesus sandals . . .

Frank   Why not?

Tony   What if somebody stamps on your toe?

Frank   I'll crucify 'em.

Tony   Sandals, that's just the pits, that is . . .

Frank   I'm playing in these and you lot can knackers.

Phil   Oh, I mean, this is just pathetic . . . we can't play with three . . .

Tony   Maybe we could ask to borrow a couple on loan for half an hour.

Frank   Yeah, a couple of props from the Cobblers.

Tony   If we run about really fast maybe they'll think there's more.

Frank   Yeah . . .

Tony   I was joking.

Frank   It's a bit desperate, really.

Phil   Did either of you train this week?

Tony   What was that?

Phil   Train . . . you know training . . .

Frank   Is that a foreign . . . ?

Phil   Try saying it . . . it's dead easy . . . training . . .

Frank   Is it French?

Tony   Tra – track . . .

Phil   No . . . training . . .

Tony   Pain . . . paining . . .

Phil   Nearly.

Tony   No, I can't say it.

Frank   I can't do it . . . the last time I trained, Queen Victoria had just died.

Tony   Last time I trained she'd just been born.

Phil   The last time I trained the earth was a gaseous mass.

Tony   Weird . . .

Steve *appears*.

Steve . . . yo . . .

Frank   Yo . . . Steve . . .

Phil   Yo . . .

Steve   Yo . . . here we go, here we go, here we go . . .

Phil   Where's the others?

Tony   Where've you been?

Steve   Got lost in Goole . . . found this great pub . . .
Theakston's Old Peculiar on draft . . .

Tony   Nice one.

Phil   Where's Tommy and Jack?

Steve   Tommy can't come and Jack's wife says he's gone
fishing.

Phil   Brilliant!

Frank   Why can't Tommy make it?

Steve   I think him and their lass have had a bit of an
argument. I could hear her shouting as I walked down the
garden so I thought I'd leave it.

Phil   Oh brilliant thinking, Steve . . . if you'd've called for
him he might have come.

Tony   If you say brilliant again I'll die.

Phil   Brilliant.

Steve   We're not going to play with just four, are we?

Frank   Are you joking . . . ? We were playing with three.

Steve   Let's leave it and get in the beer tent . . .

Frank   Get changed, it'll be a laugh.

Steve   Who for?

Tony   Upton Social Club and about a hundred and fifty spectators.

Frank   Look at it like this, if we lose it's only fifteen minutes then straight into the beer tent.

Steve   Hey, I don't like all this positive talk.

Tony   Like what?

Steve   Like *if* we lose . . . I'm more used to *when* we lose.

Phil   At least it's not raining . . .

Tony   There's a bad wind, though . . .

Steve   There's a bad wind in here. Is it you?

Tony   Is it heck.

Frank   It's that Theakston's.

Steve *is looking in his bag.*

Steve   Oh shite, man . . . I've left me shirt . . .

Phil   Oh thanks . . . that's . . .

Tony   Bloody brilliant . . .

Frank   I've got a spare one . . . (*He dips into his bag and produces a massive shirt.*) Here, get that on . . .

Steve   Oh, I can't wear that, Frank . . . I'll look like a balloon.

Tony   Get it on . . . bit of wind and you'll be laughing.

Phil   Put a shirt on, Steve, I feel sick.

Steve   Shut your moustache, will you?

Frank   Come here, let me play a tune on your ribs.

Steve *puts the shirt on.*

Steve   Look at this.

Phil   Man at Top Shop?

Tony   Wham! Jitterbug.

Frank   Man at Oxfam.

Tony   Who does the shirt belong to, Frank? Your lass?

A beat.

Phil   Oh, sore point.

Frank   That's the only bloody thing she left when she went.

Steve   Have you got a mortgage for it?

Frank   I've got some good memories of that shirt . . . we useter go camping in it.

Phil   Right, are we ready! Steve, ready?

Steve *has the shirt on but is looking for his jockstrap in his bag.*

Steve   That's not mine . . .

Tony   Well, it's not mine . . .

Phil   Come on, let's start to think about the game.

Tony   Rugby is a game played by men with odd-shaped balls.

Frank   Oh, oh . . . every one a winner. For me rugby is a game of two halves.

Tony   Give blood: play rugby.

Frank   Give orange: play squash.

Tony *groans.*

Hey, not bad, I just made that up.

Phil   Right, listen . . . are we going to play or not?

Steve   No.

Tony   Might as well . . .

Frank   We can ask to put one man in the scrum.

Steve   We're not going to do the war-chant, are we?

They perform a hideous war-chant.

Phil   Are we hell, let's just get out there . . . and get it bloody over with.

Steve   Let's get in that bloody beer tent.

They all run downstage and find a space. The weather is quite cold and they react accordingly. **Steve** *will tuck his hands right down his shorts.* **Tony** *has picked up the ball.*

Tony   Tony Burtoft. Apprentice miner. Age: twenty-two. Weight: one hundred and ninety pounds. Height: six point one. Position: centre. Hobbies: racing whippets.

The ball is thrown.

Frank   Frank Rowley. Butcher. Age: thirty-two. Weight: two hundred and fifteen pounds. Height: six point one. Position: prop. Hobbies: anything to do with my hands.

The ball is thrown.

Steve   Steve Edwards. Car mechanic. Age: twenty-five. Weight: one hundred and eighty pounds. Height: six point one. Position: loose forward. Hobbies: drinking.

The ball is thrown.

Phil   Phil Hopley. Teacher. Age: twenty-nine. Weight: one hundred and sixty pounds. Height: five point eight. Position: stand-off. Hobbies: reading, Scrabble, hunting around antique fairs on a Sunday.

Pause.

Right, here we go . . . if anyone gets the ball, this time . . . pass!

All   Oh yeah . . .

The players go upstage and freeze.

Hazel *enters.*

Hazel   I' faith, good sirs, the fools the Wheatsheaf played
And lost well bad
The largest defeat they'd ever had.
The petal-soft warriors sickened by the score,
Will in time vow to play no more
Take heed of how they've lost a game,
I' faith, good sirs, who can they blame . . . ?
Only themselves . . .
Thus Arthur's quest is harder still,
Made so by our author's quill . . .
How can they play with motive gone . . . ?
Can Arthur coax them . . . ?
Now watch on . . .

Hazel *exits.*

The players come out of their freeze. **Phil** *leaves the ball upstage.*

Phil   That is it this time and I mean it . . .

Steve   And me . . .

Phil   You? You never did a bloody thing.

Steve   Why, what did you do?

Phil   At least I moved.

Tony   Did you? I must have blinked.

Phil   Why don't you tackle, Steve?

Steve   Why don't you pass?

Phil   I did pass.

Steve   Not to me . . .

Phil   I can't pass to you unless you move on to the ball . . .
and don't stand there like a dickhead.

Frank   I think I'll have a nice big piece of T-bone when I get home . . .

Tony   I bet we'd beat 'em at darts.

Steve   Dominoes.

Frank   Drinking . . . (*He laughs.*)

Arthur *enters upstage and crouches down to the players.*

Arthur   All right, fellers?

Tony
Steve } (*together*)   All right.

Arthur   Arthur . . . Arthur Hoyle nice to meet you.

Phil   Don't tell me you're a scout for the British touring party.

Frank   Don't you mean ENSA?

Arthur   No . . . I thought you had a bit of bad luck in that game . . .

They all burst out laughing.

Steve   Hey, come on, man, fifty-four–nil in fifteen minutes, that's more than a bit of bad luck.

Tony   That's a tragedy.

Arthur   You can laugh but I thought you displayed some fine talent, some promise.

Tony   Has he got a white stick?

Frank   Has he got a brain?

Arthur   Okay, there were only four of you . . . but even so.

Phil   Yeah, well, thanks for the thoughts.

Arthur   Do you have a trainer?

Steve   Do worms have legs?

Frank We did . . . but he's gone fishing.

Arthur Look . . . I don't know how you'd feel about this, but I'd be willing to train you . . . help you out . . . I used to play a bit.

Phil No . . . er . . .

Arthur I tell you what we could do if you like . . . Give me a trial . . . Five weeks' trial . . . How about that? Just up to the next sevens.

Phil No thanks, mate . . .

Steve Hang on, Phil. How do we know that you're any good?

Arthur That's why I'm suggesting that you take me on for a five-week trial.

Frank Well, it's not for me, I've had enough.

Arthur Come on fellers, you don't mean to tell me that you're willing to pack in playing rugby as easy as that?

Frank Yeah, that's exactly what I mean.

Steve We can't even muster seven players.

Arthur That's where I come in . . . use my influence . . . pull a few strings . . .

Frank No . . . we're over the bloody hill.

Arthur (*aside*) I'll rot in hell for the lies I tell. (*To the players.*) Rubbish, over the hill . . . Look at Brian Bevan.

Frank It's too much like hard work.

Steve Yeah . . . thanks anyway.

Arthur Oh, come on lads . . . give us a break.

Tony What's in it for you?

Arthur Love of the game, that's all . . .

Phil I don't know . . .

Arthur Listen, come to training at Walton sports fields
. . . Tuesday, right? Think about it.

Phil Yeah, we will.

Steve I'm gonna think about that beer tent.

Frank Mmmm, nice idea . . .

Steve, **Phil** and **Frank** *stand to leave.*

Steve See you, Arthur, nice to meet yer . . .

They start to walk off.

Arthur Think about Tuesday, lads.

They give a disinterested 'Yeah' and exit.

Tony *remains. A beat.*

Good lads.

Tony Not bad.

Arthur Lost interest?

Tony Yeah . . . Winning's easy, innit? Losing's hard.

Arthur Don't tell me. How long have you been playing?
(*He throws the ball to* **Tony**.)

Tony Oh, a ball! Started at school.

Arthur Haven't you got any proper kit?

Tony Nobody's bothered . . . We useter pay subs but
that's died off. Did you see Frank's sandals . . . ? He's daft.
Apparently he was a right animal . . . but their lass left home
and he lost interest.

Arthur Self-respect?

Tony What?

Arthur Don't matter . . . What about the others?

Tony Phil's a decent player when he gets the right ball
. . . He's a play-maker . . . he played at college or summat in
Leicester . . . summat.

Arthur Loughborough?

Tony Yeah, I think that's it. Rugby Union.

Arthur Ay, it would be . . . whisper it.

Tony Yeah.

A beat.

Did you play?

Arthur Hey, I'm not that old.

Tony Er . . .

Arthur Hooker . . . Wakey Trinity.

Tony Whoooohhhh!

Arthur I played a couple of first-team games.

Tony Got the build for a hooker.

Arthur Yeah . . . What's happened to the other three?

Tony Hardly ever turn up.

Arthur Haven't you got any influence?

Tony No way.

Arthur You could have a word with them couldn't
you . . . ? Get them to train.

Tony I can try, but I can't promise . . .

Arthur I'll give you a couple of quid . . .

Tony What?

Arthur If you have a word . . .

Tony Yeah, can do.

Arthur   Look, here's a fiver . . . just have a word with 'em, get 'em out there on Tuesday . . .

Tony   What's it all about, this?

Arthur   I love the game, that's all, let's just say that.

Tony   You can say what you like for a fiver.

Arthur   You'll train, won't you?

Tony   Yeah.

Arthur   What do you think to the Cobblers Arms?

Music.

Tony   Brilliant.

Arthur   Do you think so?

Tony   There's not a team in the North to touch 'em . . . unbeatable . . .

Arthur   I don't know. How would you feel about playing against 'em?

Tony   They're in a different league, man, it'd be like playing against tanks.

The music fades.

Arthur   Anyway, it's only a thought . . . We can dream, can't we?

Tony   Dream we can.

Arthur   Do what you will, you know, Tuesday?

Tony   Yeah, right, I'll get off, then . . . see you . . .

Arthur   Tuesday.

Tony *exits.*

Our lass'll kill me . . .

Blackout.

She'll kill me.

Reg *enters behind* **Arthur**.

Reg I'm not a wicked man, though many say I am a bastard. I'm a fair man, I like to see fair play. Old Arthur's sweating, I can smell his pig-like stench from here. Silly sod to bet his house in such a way, and as you saw I tried to speak in sensible terms and halt his foolish gob. I wouldn't take a house, not from an ordinary bloke. I wouldn't let him choke by Doreen's hand. Here's what I'll do: I'll conjure a note, and on it I've wrote: 'It's a determined man who's bet all he's got.' I'll take three grand off you in this bet, Arthur, pal. Don't want to see a proud man out of house and home.

Arthur Three grand, Reg.

Reg In cash, I like cash. What the hell would I do with your hovel, anyway?

Arthur Yeah, right, thanks Reg.

Reg How's the training going, Arthur?

Arthur Great.

Reg Yeah?

Arthur Couldn't be better.

Reg Lads eager, are they?

Arthur Yeah . . . As soon as I put the prospect to them they almost bit my hand off.

Reg Really?

Arthur Have you made enquiries about the draw?

Reg You leave that to me . . . I'm even thinking of giving you a bye to the final . . . Make it more of a prestige game for your lads . . . Don't want to leave 'em with nothing.

Arthur Yeah . . . right . . .

Reg Just make sure that you've got a team . . . otherwise it could be embarrassing.

The light goes out on **Reg**, *who exits.*

Arthur *takes off his anorak through the ensuing speech. He wears a rugby shirt under his coat. A rugby ball is thrown on to him. He looks around for the players to appear.*

Arthur Tuesday night I waited and waited . . . Walton sports field was a desert of green, with not a player to be seen at all . . .

Hazel *enters and sits on a bench.*

Hazel My Lords, on Walton fields he stood in storms and
    hail,
And blowing gales the like of which would crack your
    cheeks,
Which you have heard from tales.
Every hour he stood alone the stronger grew his cause,
More determined was his soaking gait.
But still his part was to wait . . . and wait . . .
His thoughts lay with success,
He knew he dare not fail . . .
And as he stood drenched on yon fair fields . . .
The rest were supping ale . . .

Downstage are **Frank** *and* **Phil** *with a drink of beer. They have had a few.*

Phil Oh funny . . . honestly funny . . . some of the things they come out with, honestly funny.

Frank Yeah?

Phil Oh yeah . . .

Frank Like what?

Phil Oh, all sorts . . . I mean, stories in the staff-room, funny.

Frank Yeah, yeah . . . like what?

Phil   Like this kid writes, William the Conqueror's first name was Norman.

This meets with death.

Frank (*taking a drink*)   Oh yeah.

Phil (*undaunted*)   Funny . . . and this lad says . . . No, I can't tell you, it's sick.

Frank   Tell us, Phil man.

Phil   No, it'll upset you, it's sick . . . you're a man of sensibilities, you're a sensitive man, Frank . . .

Frank   I cut dead meat up . . . I'd hardly call that sensitive.

Phil   So . . . I've got this class . . . a couple of years ago . . . and this has just come to me . . . we're talking about the Ripper . . .

Frank   Yeah . . . yeah . . .

Phil   A slow-learning group . . . reading and writing problems . . .

Frank   Like me . . .

Phil   And we're trying to diagnose what to do with the Yorkshire Ripper.

Frank   Yeah, go on . . .

Phil   And this little lad says . . . 'Sir?'

Frank   Yeah . . .

Phil   'Sir, I know what we could do with the Yorkshire Ripper' . . . I says, 'Great, go on, Stuart . . . what would you do?' Then he says . . . 'I'd send him to America.'

Frank (*beginning to laugh*)   Norman the Conqueror . . .

Frank *and* **Phil** *begin to cackle and then the cackling subsides. They both sigh . . . drink their beer.*

Blackout on **Frank** *and* **Phil**. *A light on* **Arthur**.

Arthur   And I'm waiting and waiting.

The lights come up on **Frank** *and* **Phil**.

Phil   What do you think to this Arthur bloke?

Frank   He's got a painting and decorating firm, I've seen his van . . . Decent player in his day.

Phil   Could be handy, could that . . . I want my living-room Artexing.

Frank   What do you reckon about *this* lot . . . ?

Phil   I don't know . . .

Frank   He's keen . . .

Phil   If he's out on Walton sports field by himself he is keen. He'll be arrested for loitering.

Frank   Wonder who turned up?

Phil   I could guess . . .

Frank   Not Steve . . .

Phil   No chance . . . he'll be trying to pick something up.

Frank   He ought to pick something up, incurable.

Phil   Tony'll turn out.

Frank   Yeah . . . mate I was talking to yesterday reckons this Arthur's a weird bloke . . . says his brain's in a box somewhere.

Phil   Yeah?

Frank   Hard case.

Phil   Just let him start with me.

Frank   And me . . .

Phil   I'll tell him where to get off . . . Listen, you couldn't see your way to letting me have another batch of them Tbones, could you? You know those you got off the back of a warehouse?

Frank   Yeah, come and pick them up . . . and bring a few mags with you . . .

Phil   You dirty sod.

Frank   Where do you get them from?

Phil   All over the place, you never know when they're gonna show up. The other day we were reading *Women in Love*, this fifth-year lad whips out this porno book. 'Look at this, sir,' he says. 'This is women in love' . . . I'd never seen anything like it . . . I gave him a dressing down, made him feel embarrassed and confiscated the magazine, told him I was going to burn it.

Frank   And did you?

Phil   Did I hell . . . I kept it . . . it was a classic . . . I'll bring it down.

Frank   If you would . . . Another drink?

Phil   How many's this?

Frank   This is six . . .

Phil   Yeah, go on, then, I haven't got far to walk . . .

Frank   No?

Phil   No, only to the car . . . (*He drinks and hands* **Frank** *his glass.*) Cheers.

Blackout. A light on **Hazel**.

Hazel   Yet still alone, and with his thoughts only, he sat there bald and wet, and yet the wind and rain had ceased and all the air was clear . . . He turned his mind to lofty thoughts of subjects he held dear.

A light comes up on **Arthur**.

Arthur This never happens in *Rocky* . . . I love *Rocky*, me.
I've seen them all, *Rocky One*, *Two* and *Three*. I like *Rocky Two*
the best, you know where Adrian's dying in hospital and
Rocky's there with his trainer, and she just moves her
fingers and says, 'Win, Rocky, win.' Oh, I was just stood in
the cinema, shouting. I felt a right fart, and when I looked
around everybody else was shouting and all.

The light goes out on **Arthur**.

Hazel And so the time has come and on this stage, good
sirs, needs must I play my part, and meet our hero face to
face. The sands of time run fast . . . five weeks is but a blink
in the history of our globe. Arthur's quest is waning and Reg
has his team in training. (**Hazel** *drops into a press-up position
and begins to perform press-ups with ease.*)

Arthur Not bad . . .

Hazel Eh?

Arthur Pretty impressive.

Hazel If you're a flasher, I'm not interested.

Arthur You what?

Hazel If you're one of those little men who hangs about
flashing his wares, I'm not interested.

Arthur I'm not a flasher . . . I'm training . . .

Hazel Training . . . ugh?

Arthur My lads are on a five-mile run . . . (*Aside.*) I'll rot
in hell for the lies I tell.

Hazel And you're the first one back?

Arthur Sharp . . . very sharp . . .

Hazel Oh, trainer eh . . . ? I didn't realise.

Arthur Been jogging, have you?

Hazel Yeah. Light jog . . . I've just had a heavy session.

Arthur   Husband at home, then, is he . . . ?

Hazel   Don't come the crudity with me fatty, you're barking up the wrong tree.

Arthur   Oh, I stand corrected.

Hazel   Weights . . . I train with weights . . .

Arthur   A couple of bags of sugar on the end of a broom handle?

Hazel   Oh, I can see that you're fit . . . every curve in your physique screams out . . . fitness . . . How often do you train – once a year?

Arthur   Ha ha . . . very funny . . .

Hazel   You men make me laugh . . .

Arthur   That's hard . . . I bet . . . seeing you . . .

Hazel   I see them like you down at the club, a game of squash, a sauna, twenty cigs, and a heart attack . . . Rugby players are the worst. Training session and then seven pints of Guinness . . . Fitness . . . you don't know what fitness is . . .

Arthur   Here, catch . . .

Arthur *throws the ball quite hard but she catches it easily. Through this speech they continue to pass the ball.*

Where's this club, then?

Hazel   Above the supermarket?

Arthur   Oh yeah . . .

Hazel   Showers . . . sauna . . . solarium, loose weights . . . getting some Nautilus at Christmas.

Arthur   How much is it, then?

Hazel   Interested, are you?

Arthur   Only making conversation . . .

Hazel   You could have a free trial.

Arthur   Who owns it?

Hazel   A woman called Hazel Scott . . .

Arthur   Dave Scott's wife . . . the international scrum half . . .

Hazel   That's right . . . we separated two years ago . . . Give me a ring if you're interested . . . we're in the *Yellow Pages* . . . I'll show you what training is . . .

Arthur   I doubt it . . .

Hazel   If I was you, I'd start to worry about your team . . . I think they must have got lost . . .

Arthur   Now I can see why your husband left you . . .

Hazel   I left him . . .

Hazel *exits, taking the ball with her. She reaches a side of the stage and does a perfect reverse pass.*

Arthur *catches it . . . and follows her off.*

Arthur   Not bad . . . hey, listen . . .

Arthur *exits.*

The lights go down, then come up again.

Steve *comes on, wearing a pair of overalls. He lies down and is looking under a car.* **Phil** *follows, wearing a tracksuit, and then* **Frank***, in his butcher's togs. Their speeches overlap, and their actions are done to the audience.*

Steve   I think that what you've got is a fracture on a brake pipe . . . fluids escaping, and you need new shock absorbers on both the front sides. Apart from that, and a dicky front light, the car's fine.

Phil   The kestrel is, of course, not only a real feature in Casper's life, but it also serves as a symbol of the freedom that Casper will never have himself until he manages to escape from the environment that he currently finds himself caged in.

Frank   I can't really let you have that for less than two pound. It's best rump steak, you see . . . I've got to make a living. Tell you what . . . give us one-ninety.

Arthur *enters upstage.*

Arthur   Oi!

All   Sorry, what did you say . . . Sir?/Lad?/Love?

Arthur   Oi, it's me . . .

They all look around for **Arthur***, who has invaded their very privacy.*

All   What?

Arthur   What happened . . . ?

All   What?

Arthur   What happened on Tuesday, lads, eh?

All   Not here, I'm busy . . .

Arthur   I said . . . what bloody happened?

All (*whispering*)   Go away.

Arthur   No.

All   Look, this is very embarrassing . . . sorry . . . Sir/Class/Love . . .

Arthur   Come tomorrow . . . Walton fields . . .

All   Go away . . .

Arthur   Tomorrow?

All   All right . . .

Arthur   See you tomorrow, then . . .

Arthur *goes. General cover lights.*

Phil   Now soon to sing their songs of old,

    Their battle chants of war,
    So let music play and voices swell
    And sunken hearts rise from dark hell.

Steve, **Frank** *and* **Phil** *take off their outer clothes, revealing training gear, tracksuits, etc.*

Hey, Frank . . . 'She was poor but she was honest.' (*He sings.*) 'She was poor but she was honest . . . Victim of a rich man's whim . . .'

All (*singing*)   First he ****** her, then he left her,
    And she had a child by him.
    It's the same the whole world over . . .
    It's the poor what gets the blame . . .
    It's the rich what gets the pleasure
    And it's all the bloody same . . .

Tony *enters, in training gear.*

Steve   Hey up . . . Club song . . . 'Blackbird' . . .

Frank   Which version . . . clean or filthy . . . ?

Tony   Filthy . . .

Phil   You lot are worse than the kids at school.

Tony   We are kids . . .

Steve   Some of us . . .

Tony   Ooohh, getting all defensive, just because you shave . . . don't come all macho . . .

Steve   Oh big word for an apprentice miner i'n't?

Tony   Here's another big word . . .

Steve   What?

Tony   Eat shit, you skinny gett!

Frank   I love the humour . . .

Steve   'Blackbird' . . . Club song by Steve Edwards . . . Mr Hopley, sir . . .

Phil   Is it one of your own compositions, lad?

Steve   Yes sir . . . It's taken me years of creative turmoil and anguish . . .

Phil   Right, let's hear it, lad, if it's any good you can put it in your sixteen-plus English file . . .

Steve   Once a boy was no good . . . took a girl into a wood . . .

Frank   Bye bye blackbird . . .

Steve   Laid her down upon the grass . . .
Pinched her tits and slapped her arse . . .

All   Bye bye blackbird . . .

Steve   Took her where nobody else could find her . . .
To a place where he could really grind her . . .
Rolled her over on her front . . .
Shoved his . . .

All   Yo . . .

Steve   Right up her . . .

All   Ears . . . Blackbird bye bye . . .

Phil   Give me the other version, any day . . .

Steve   Boring . . .

Frank   Three out of ten . . .

Tony   One out of twenty from the Russian judge . . .

Phil (*in a French accent*)   Luxembourg . . . nil points . . .

Tony   Get this one going . . . ba da da . . . ba da da . . .

They do a rendition of the Flying Pickets: 'Spring is in the Air' . . . It is a common impersonation of the Flying Pickets.

As they sing, **Arthur** *enters with a number of rugby balls under his arms. He throws the balls to the lads.*

Arthur   Catch . . . What have we got here, 'Opportunity Knocks'?

Frank   Just having a song . . .

Arthur   If you want to sing, you're in the wrong game . . .

Phil   Just a laugh . . .

Arthur   Just . . . let's have a word . . . I don't want to waste time. Tonight we'll work on general fitness . . . cardiovascularity.

Steve   I think my tea's ready . . .

Tony   Shurrup.

Steve   Don't start . . .

Arthur   Ball-handling . . . and the speed of moving the ball from the . . . play the ball . . .

Phil   We know all this . . .

Arthur   I'm assuming you know nothing . . .

Tony   He doesn't . . .

Phil   Piss off . . .

Tony   Touchy . . .

Arthur   I want to know if you've ever had any set moves, from penalties . . . or from scrumming . . .

Phil   What about other players . . . ?

Arthur   That's my worry . . . I'll be playing hooker for a start . . .

Steve   Can you hook?

Arthur   You'll have to wait and see . . .

Tony   What time'll we finish?

Arthur   Why?

Steve   He's got to be in bed . . .

Frank   With their lass . . .

Tony   I don't want to be late . . .

Frank   Nor me . . .

Arthur   Look, let's just make a start . . . Right . . . let's have a run.

Frank   A what?

Arthur   Start off with three miles . . . just to get warm.

Steve   Warm . . . ?

Frank   No . . . I'm not running about . . . I've been on my feet all day at work . . . I'll have a game of touch and pass . . .

Arthur   It's only a short run, Frank.

Frank   I don't want to overdo it, I want to be able to walk tomorrow.

Phil   Come on Frank . . . take it steady . . .

Arthur   Look, it's not a race . . . it's just a matter of finishing . . . Don't you watch the London Marathon?

Frank   Watch, yeah . . .

Tony   Let's get summat done . . . I'm gonna miss 'Top of the Pops' at this rate . . .

Frank   Oh, come on, then . . .

They all stand in a line across the stage. Those not talking make a heavy breathing and plodding noise . . . (sub-Berkoff).

Steve   Out we went . . . over the crisp grass of Walton fields . . . Down the slope which led to the main road . . .

Phil   Through the gate . . . and on to the pavement . . .

Tony   The change of running surface . . . jarred . . .

Steve   Arthur led . . .

Frank   And we like warriors followed bunched behind him . . .

Steve   The night was drawing in . . .

Arthur   It wasn't dark but . . . it would be in the hour . . .

Phil   Car side lights were beginning to ease their way effortlessly towards us . . .

Tony   Sodium street lights sparkled to life . . .

Steve   As we hit a hump-backed bridge . . . the weariness . . . the fatigue . . .

Phil   The complete and utter lack of fitness was beginning to register in us all . . .

Steve   My legs felt heavy . . . calves aching . . . a hard pounding drumming reverberating up my back . . .

Tony   The bridge brow was in sight and then the descent . . .

Frank   Twenty yards of easy running . . .

Arthur   I didn't realise that three miles was so long . . .

Frank   Saliva dripping from my mouth like a hungry dog . . . and I was aware of the effort of moving my frame . . .

Steve   The dread of meeting pedestrians loomed . . .

Phil   And mannequins . . . grinning, smirking their smug sickly expressions . . .

Steve   Their form is constant . . .

Frank   They never change . . . age leaves them untouched . . .

Tony   Our tracks rumbled along the tarmac . . .

Phil   The sight of people . . . and the impulse to make more effort to push harder . . .

Arthur Fifty-five minutes . . . for three miles a slow pace
. . . but a lot of meat in the pack . . . we returned with the
light fading . . .

They are all exhausted and collapse where they are.

Get your breath . . . All right, Frank . . . ?

Frank Just about . . . feel a bit sick . . .

Frank Deep breaths, Frank son . . .

Frank I'm okay . . .

Steve Nice one, Frankie . . .

Frank I bet I can't move tomorrow . . .

Arthur You will . . . same again tomorrow . . .

Phil What next, Arthur?

Frank That'll do for me . . .

Phil Not bad for a start. I'm about as fit as D. H.
Lawrence.

Arthur I think he's dead.

Phil That's what I mean.

Steve Nice and easy session . . . pass me the Guinness
drip, will you . . . ?

Tony Enjoyed it . . .

Steve I have.

Phil You're not a bad bloke, are you Arthur?

Arthur Aren't I?

Phil No, you're all right, mate, all right . . . I had my
doubts . . . but you're an honest man . . . I can smell a
crook, but you're okay . . .

Arthur Thanks . . .

Phil I mean it . . .

Tony   Yeah . . . and me . . .

Frank   Do you know what our training amounted to in the past? We'd meet in the Wheatsheaf . . . have about six pints, pick thirteen men . . .

Steve   If thirteen ever turned up . . .

Frank   Then it was back to my place to watch the videos . . .

Arthur   I love *Rocky* . . . *One*, *Two* and *Three* . . .

Phil   Pulp crap . . .

Arthur   Oh, Barry friggin' Norman now, are we . . . ?

Steve   Hey, we had some laughs. Can you remember that time when Jack's cousin said that he wanted a game . . . turned up, played and got his earlobe bit off.

Frank   He played well . . .

Phil   We only lost thirty–nil that game.

Arthur   No more losing talk . . . think positive. I want to succeed.

Tony   I know what'll succeed: a budgie with no teeth.

Phil   That's the sort of comment this team doesn't need.

Steve   Let's not get into it tonight, eh?

Frank   Yeah . . .

Steve   Can you remember when I broke my hand?

Tony   You didn't do that playing rugby.

Phil   That's true.

Steve   I'll tell you what I did do. I shat into my shorts once.

Blackout. They freeze. **Arthur** *stands behind them in overhead light.*

Arthur   Ar . . . you're good lads, honest, no edge to you
. . . you love needling each other. The only thing you have
in common is the game . . . I feel a right prat, you've taken
to me, and you don't know why I'm doing all this. In any
case I don't think about it much . . . only at nights . . . I lay
awake . . .

The lights come up.

Steve   Get away man . . . I don't believe you.

Phil   It's true, and she married his brother-in-law's
nephew . . .

Frank   What did Jack say?

Phil   What would you say . . . ?

Steve   She looks like a really nice lass and all.

Arthur   I tell you what . . . let's get down to the
Wheatsheaf and have a pint, shall we?

Tony   Sounds like a good idea.

Steve   That's the sort of training I like, Arthur.

Phil   What about the fitness . . . ?

Arthur   Look at it like this . . . it's a celebration . . . all I
want to do is to show my gratitude to you lot for turning out
for training.

Frank   You had to twist our arms a bit, though.

Phil   I nearly had a fit when you came into school, the
kids went wild . . .

Arthur   I think it's the head . . .

Phil   Probably . . .

Arthur   Well, what do you say, then . . . ? A swift five
down the Wheatsheaf Arms? I'll get the first round in.

Steve   I'll drink to that . . .

Frank   And me . . .

A change of lighting. The players set up the gymnasium with the following equipment: lat machine, exercise bike, bench press, hack-squat, sit-ups bench, step-up bench.

Steve *exits.*

Hazel *enters.*

Hazel   And so to play a major part within this vasty 'O'. Arthur trained with just one jog, his players' skills, well, naff, he could have laughed but took them for a drink of sack. Now remember how on Walton fields came the offer of a club. It was training that would win the day, not supping in the pub. Thus Hazel takes the boards once more, training in her gym, all plush and modern and well equipped; well fit athletes train, and gross obese men slim. But soft . . .

The players chuckle with glee.

For as we speak, the tissue paper gladiators approach, led by their hero our coach. How will they fair with yon weights? The training will be tough. I see a question on yon fair face, sirs, are they man enough? (*She proceeds to the sit-ups bench and begins exercising.*)

The players have frozen at the back of the stage.

Tony   Hey, not bad.

Frank   Nice work.

Phil   Arthur, who's that?

Arthur   Ar, right. Hazel, can I introduce you to the team . . . ?

Hazel   Yeah.

Arthur   This is Tony, Phil, Frank.

Hazel   Hello. Come to have a go at getting fit, have you?

Tony   Yeah.

Hazel   How are the ten-mile runs?

Frank   What?

Arthur   Great, thanks.

Hazel   It's going to be hard slog . . . over the next twelve sessions.

Tony   Yeah . . .

Phil   Be gentle with us . . .

Hazel (*to the audience*)   I took them around each machine, explaining its function and explaining some common fallacies about weight-training. I could see at a glance that they were sceptical, to say the least.

Phil *is on the exercise bike.*

Phil (*whispering*)   She's not training us, is she?

Arthur   In a word?

Phil   In a word . . .

Arthur   Yes.

Frank   Great stuff.

Phil   You're joking.

Tony   He is.

Arthur   I'm not . . .

Phil   She's a woman . . .

Arthur   I thought you were educated . . .

Phil   I am . . .

Arthur   She's probably twice as fit as you . . .

Tony   No way . . .

Arthur   Just give it a go . . .

Frank   I'm not bothered . . . It's a good idea.

Phil   I'll just feel uncomfortable . . .

Arthur   She's useter training men . . .

Tony   Tell us another.

Arthur   It's her gym . . . she got body-builders 'n' all sorts of athletes coming there and she trains 'em . . .

Phil   I still say it's a bit much . . .

Hazel *goes up to* **Phil**.

Hazel   That's for women.

Embarrassed reaction from **Phil**. *The others laugh.*

Phil   Obviously . . .

Steve *enters, late.*

Steve   Oh yes, what is this . . . luxury a-go-go?

Arthur   Hazel, this is Steve . . .

Steve   Hazel . . . nice to meet you . . .

Hazel   Hello . . .

Steve   Do you have a nut in every bite . . . ?

Hazel   Humorous as well, isn't he . . . ?

Steve   Not funny but fast . . .

Hazel   Okay then, warm-up on the bike . . . let's make a start . . . We'll start with a circuit . . . Arthur . . . legs, Frank sit-ups, Tony lats . . . Phil bench . . . we're looking –

Arthur   I feel like I've shit my pants . . .

Hazel   I'm waiting . . .

Arthur   Sorry . . .

Hazel   We're looking for quick ten reps, make sure that the movement is strict, do not cheat . . . if it's too light don't worry, it'll serve as a warm-up exercise, and go . . .

Steve   Hey, look at this . . . I love it . . . this is about my standard.

Each man begins to exercise . . . The weights clunk about. **Hazel** *watches.* **Steve** *fools . . .*

Hazel   Concentrate on the movements . . .

Steve   Anybody want anything bringing from the shops . . . ? 'Riding along on a push-bike, honey . . .' Ho ah ho ah . . . (*He starts to make hand signals . . . and banks the bike.*) Get out of the way . . .

Hazel   Come on, cut it out . . .

Steve   Get out of the way . . .

Hazel   Very funny, now pack it in.

Hazel *looks around the gym and sees all the lads on the machines, performing the exercises pathetically. She is very displeased.*

All right, change . . .

They all change. **Arthur** *bangs the leg machine.*

Don't bang the weights.

The lads move to a different machine. **Hazel** *gives them the go-ahead. They begin work on the machines. The effect is comic (and much improvising of the comic elements of the machines should be allowed).* **Hazel** *goes around to the various machines and encourages the lads to perform correctly.* **Tony** *is performing a neck-press with the weight to his head.*

Tony   This one hurts your head.

Hazel *encourages* **Frank** *on the hack-squat.*

Frank   It's not very good for my piles.

Hazel *gets them to change machines. A lighting change.*

Hazel (*sitting on the bike*)   I worked them slowly to begin with. I could see that they were desperately out of shape –

All the lads perform one exercise.

– and to give them their due, they played their part. We trained for a full week, split system, and Arthur would work at the back of the gym on ball skills.

The lads perform two repeats of the exercise.

As we got into week three it was time to push them. (*To the players.*) By the time we're finished you'll be doing thirty reps each.

All   Thirty?

The players become more motivated and begin to count to themselves. **Hazel** *is still encouraging their work. They count to thirty and as they count the volume increases, so by the time they reach thirty they are completely shouting.*

Blackout.

Act Two

The players are still counting. **Hazel** *walks around, encouraging them.*

Hazel Come on, pull . . . !

Steve Get off.

Hazel No, pull . . . good . . .

Tony *is on lats.*

Pull . . .

Tony I can't . . . pull . . .

Hazel Force it . . . pull . . . just your back . . . good . . .

Arthur *is doing step-ups on the bench.*

How many, Arthur?

Arthur Twenty.

Hazel Another . . . ten.

Arthur No, I'm knackered . . . I want a rest . . .

Hazel Another ten . . . come on . . . I'll count you . . . one . . . two . . . three . . . four . . . five . . . six . . .

Arthur I'm gonna spew . . .

Hazel Two more . . . one . . . two . . . good . . .

Arthur Oh shit . . .

Arthur *dashes off-stage to be sick.*

Hazel Listen, lads . . . listen . . . a minute . . . Phil, Tony. You've really got to go for it now, you've really got to push it . . . push to the limits of the pain barrier . . . otherwise the training's pointless.

Frank It's no good, I've had enough . . .

Hazel   You've got to go more, Frank . . . hit the wall and straight out the other side . . . that's what it's about fellers . . .

Steve   Can we just have a minute . . . ?

Hazel   Okay, a timed minute . . . starting now . . .

They all relax. **Hazel** *times them.*

Phil   Do you get something sexual out of all this?

Hazel   Don't talk shit . . . forty seconds . . .

Phil   You're a sadist . . . aren't you? Go on, admit it . . .

Hazel   Thirty seconds . . .

Tony   This is harder than pit work . . .

Steve   You're never there in any case . . .

Tony   I am when we're working . . .

Hazel   Fifteen . . .

Frank   Where's Arthur?

Hazel   Being sick . . . time, lads . . . a minute . . . back you get . . .

Phil   No, hang on . . . have another minute . . .

Hazel   No come on . . .

Tony   Wait on a bit, Hazel . . .

Hazel   You said a minute . . .

Phil   Not a literal minute, a minute as in five minutes . . .

Hazel   Get back on these exercises, all of you . . .

Steve   No . . . have a minute, man, for God's sake . . .

Frank   In a tick . . .

Hazel   Now . . .

Phil   We've been doing all the work . . . it's easy to shout at people, I should know, I'm a teacher.

Hazel   Okay . . . if you want to take that attitude, fair enough . . .

Frank   Thanks . . .

Phil   We'll train again in five or ten . . .

Hazel   When your muscles have grown cold?

Tony   Sarcasm . . .

Steve   The lowest form of . . .

Hazel   That's okay by me, it's your money, I suppose.

Tony   Eh?

A beat.

Steve   You what?

Phil   What is . . . ?

Hazel   All this training going to waste . . . it's a waste of your money.

Tony   Have we got to pay for all this?

Hazel   No . . . this is free . . . the bet, I mean . . .

Phil   What are you on about . . . ?

Steve   What bet?

Hazel   You're not that thick . . . come on . . .

Phil   What's all this about a bet?

Hazel   Okay, forget it . . . let's get back to work . . .

Frank   No . . . hang on, I smell something a bit fishy . . .

Steve   I think it's Tony . . .

Tony   Bollocks you . . .

Phil   Is this summat to do with Arthur?

Hazel   I really don't know.

Tony   Come on, leave it . . . it's got nothing to do with us . . .

Arthur *enters.*

Arthur   Jesus Christ . . . I've just thrown half my insides up . . . what's got nothing to do with you, Tony . . . ?

Tony   This bet . . .

Arthur   No . . . right . . . Come on, let's push on . . .

Phil   I want to know about this bet, Arthur . . .

Frank   Yeah, how does it affect us . . . ?

Arthur   Who told you?

Hazel   I thought they knew . . .

Arthur   They do now . . .

Steve   What is it . . . top secret or something?

Arthur   Right . . . I suppose I'd better tell you . . .

Hazel   I think you'd better . . . before we go any further.

Arthur   Sit down lads, this might hurt . . .

Frank   Us or you?

Arthur   Both . . .

They all sit down.

So I told them about the bet . . . and they were quite amiable about it . . . Steve offered to put some money against them winning . . .

Steve   I'll have twenty quid against us Arth . . .

Arthur   We haven't got a chance, they said . . . they were right . . .

Tony   We haven't got a chance . . .

Arthur They didn't like Reg Welsh, that was clear . . .

Steve He's a bastard . . . and a crook . . . take that from me . . . I did his car once . . . he never paid me . . . sent two of his thugs around . . .

Arthur That's the way Reg works . . .

Frank It makes no difference anyway . . . if we enter we might not get drawn against the Cobblers in any case . . . we'll still probably go out in the first round.

Arthur I had to tell them it'd all been set up, that Reg had arranged for us to have a bye . . . so we'd meet in the final . . . that went down like a fart at a wedding . . .

Tony You what?

Steve It's set up?

Arthur That's what I said . . .

Phil Why us?

Tony Yeah . . .

Frank We've never bloody won a game . . .

Steve No . . . never will . . .

Phil Oh yeah . . . I'm beginning to see it all . . . you and Reg Welsh must have had a good laugh about us . . . eh? Is that it? The Wheatsheaf . . . the joke side . . . the side who play with four men . . . is that it?

Tony Right . . . I'm not flogging my heart out for you to win three thousand . . . not to be made a laughing stock . . . for the likes of Reg Welsh . . .

Arthur What have you got to lose . . . ? It's my money . . .

Frank It's your money, but it's our pride . . . We've had enough jibes shoved down our throats without being set up against the best side in Yorkshire . . . We want to win for a change . . .

Arthur   This is your chance . . .

Phil   Rubbish, that's utter rubbish and you know it. I'm off . . . Come on, Steve . . .

Steve   I'm coming . . .

Arthur   Listen . . .

Tony   No . . . you've got yourself in this shit . . . you get yourself out of it . . . don't get us involved . . .

Frank   So Reg Welsh thinks we're a joke team, does he . . . ?

Arthur   Listen, Frank . . .

Frank   Well that's fine by me . . . We are a bloody joke team . . . The game's off . . . You tell him . . . see if he finds it funny . . .

Frank *leaves upstage, singing 'Swing low, Sweet Chariot'.*

All the rest collect their belongings and leave.

Hazel *and* **Arthur** *are left.*

Hazel   Sorry . . .

Arthur   Ar . . .

Hazel   I er . . .

Arthur   Doesn't matter . . .

Hazel   I thought they knew . . .

Arthur   They had to know, I suppose . . .

Hazel   Why didn't you tell them?

Arthur   I wouldn't have got them this far . . . The mention of the Cobblers and legs turn to water . . .

Hazel   Can you blame them?

Arthur   No . . .

Hazel   Well then . . . do you want a drink?

Arthur   No . . . I feel physically and morally sick . . .

Hazel   Have another word with them . . .

Arthur   No . . .

Hazel   Why?

Arthur   Funny . . .

Hazel   What?

Arthur   I suppose Reg was right . . . said I'd seen too many *Rocky* films . . . where the underdog always wins . . .

Hazel   It's nice to think about . . . nice ideal . . .

Arthur   That's all it is . . . an ideal . . .

Hazel   We need that sort of thing . . . to escape to . . .

Arthur   Life's a bastard when you stop to think about it . . .

Hazel   Nobody wins . . .

Arthur   Ar well . . . that's my bank savings down the friggin' shoot.

Hazel   He'll take the money, then?

Arthur   Every last penny . . . plus the fact that I'll be the laughing stock . . .

Hazel   So that's my part of the bargain wrapped up too, I suppose . . .

Arthur   'Fraid so . . .

Hazel   Another icon shattered . . .

Arthur   You what?

Hazel   Broken dream . . .

Arthur   Ar . . .

Hazel   Oh well . . .

Arthur   I'd like to be able to blame somebody . . . but I can't . . .

Hazel   What are you going to do?

Arthur   Ever heard of suicide . . . ?

Hazel   Don't be stupid . . .

Arthur   I think I'll just stay here for a bit . . . if that's all right with you . . .

Hazel   Stay as long as you like . . . I'm going to nip down to the bank.

Arthur   Me too . . .

Hazel *exits*.

Have you ever been out of your mind,
And a scream of some kind . . .
Would be something obscene . . .
I feel like that now the day's at a close . . .
I knew that it wouldn't work out, I suppose . . .
And so as they all say . . . to you, adieu and farewell . . .
. . . and for the lies that I've told?
I'll go rot in hell.

He gets up slowly and begins to leave.

Tony *comes into the gym and begins to train.* **Steve** *enters and gets on the bike.* **Frank** *and* **Phil** *follow and start their exercises.*

Phil   Oi, fat bald bastard!

Arthur   Eh!

Phil   Get training, it's on . . .

Arthur   It's not . . .

Tony   It is . . .

Steve   So get moving . . .

Frank   Come on, Arthur, move it . . .

Phil If we win we split the cash . . . If we lose . . . it's all yours . . .

Arthur It's a deal . . . and listen lads . . . thanks.

Blackout.

A spotlight picks out **Hazel** *as she enters.*

Hazel The harder they trained the more single-minded they became, for the next three weeks they worked . . . and strained and pained and planed the gained muscular power . . . into shape, resilient and every hour . . . they could, they knew they should, devote their time to the cause of winning. To the front page clause: 'The Wheatsheaf beat the Cobblers out of Castleford.' . . . it was a tabloid dream, from a team that have schemed to pass and switch the ball, to play all fair and give the ground a swift turn of stud . . . They would if they could, give the ball some air . . . to turn defence to blunders with overlaps and scissor moves and lofty up 'n' unders of a genre not seen for years. Above all else, determined not to lose . . . they chose to fight, though as you've seen upon this stage they've had the right for flight . . . to withdraw . . . let brass bands be heard and battle cries of awe ring from Hull to Featherstone . . . And let our heroes know that they are not alone . . . in their struggle to be kings on a paper throne . . . Five weeks now gone . . . The Wheatsheaf mean to see their form . . . We see them now . . . Still before the storm . . .

The lights come up. The players are slowly finishing their exercises. They are tired and drop to a resting place. **Hazel** *walks around and gives them a towel. They sit still and sweating . . . quiet . . . breathing heavily . . . They remain silent. Then:*

Phil Hey!

Arthur What?

Phil Do you want to hear a poem I've written about the game?

Tony No . . .

Phil   It's good listen . . . It's a rip-off from Shakespeare . . .

Steve   Ronny Shakespeare used to do the washing for my mam . . .

Phil   Prologue *Romeo and Juliet* . . . it's taken from . . .

Frank   Very good . . .

Phil   Listen, you philistines . . . you'll get this . . . it's good:
  Two clubs each unlike in dignity,
  In fair Castleford where we'll lay our scene,
  A stupid bet, a bigotry . . .
  A grim determination to win a match so keen . . .

What do you reckon?

Tony   Brilliant . . .

Phil   'Bigotry' doesn't really work . . . but I couldn't think of another word.

Steve   How about pillock?

Phil   No . . . it doesn't even work as a half-rhyme.

Tony   Bloody hell!

Arthur   Yeah.

Frank   Knackered . . .

Steve   I feel drained . . .

Hazel   You've done well . . . should be pleased with yourselves . . . I'll put the showers on . . .

Hazel *exits*.

Tony   No shower for me . . . straight down home.

Steve   Early to bed . . .

Phil   Yeah . . .

Arthur   No . . . not for me . . .

Frank   Why not?

Arthur   I can't sleep unless I've had a drink . . .

Phil   You're in a bad way . . .

Arthur   If I don't have a couple of pints I just lie looking at the lampshade.

Steve   I'll join you for a pint in the Sheaf, Arth . . .

Arthur   Right . . . a couple of pints, fish and chips . . . then up the wooden hill to Bedfordshire . . .

Frank   Sounds like Tupper of the Track . . .

Arthur   Working-class hero . . .

Frank   True enough . . .

Arthur   Born with a silver knife in his back . . .

Steve   I feel right nervous . . .

Tony   I don't feel too bad . . . I will do tomorrow . . . I'll shit myself.

Steve   Take some extra shorts, then.

A beat.

Phil   Arthur?

Arthur   What?

Phil   At the risk of sounding pedantic . . .

All   Whoooo . . . !

Tony   Get a big sign . . . 'Sage at work'.

Phil   All right, point taken.

Steve   Brilliant.

Tony   Oh yeah, brilliant . . . brilliant . . .

Arthur   Go on . . .

Phil   I don't suppose you've overlooked the fact that we've still got only five players . . . ?

Arthur   In the nineteen fourteen Rourke's Drift test Britain only had ten men . . . and still beat a side of thirteen.

Phil   That's little comfort.

Arthur   Don't worry . . .

Frank   Have you got it in hand . . . as they say . . . ?

Arthur   I've made some arrangements . . . Right, I'm down the showers and into the Wheatsheaf for a skinful . . .

Phil   Who's taking Steve and Frankie tomorrow?

Arthur   Me . . . I'll pick you up about half-ten, Frankie?

Frank   Yeah . . .

Arthur   I'll make arrangements later, Steve . . .

Steve   Hang on, I'm coming . . . See you in Castleford lads . . .

All   Right-oh . . .

Frank   Castleford here we come . . .

Steve   Frankie goes to Castleford . . . eh hear that . . . ?

Tony   Piss off . . .

Steve   Tony's good at one-liners.

Steve *and* **Arthur** *leave,* **Steve** *singing 'Relax'.*

Tony   I don't think all this health food's been good for me.

Phil   How come?

Tony   I'm on the toilet all the time.

Frank   It's good that, clear you out . . .

Tony   I don't know about that . . . I feel like one long tube from mouth to arse.

Phil   Oesophagus . . .

Tony   Oh ar . . .

A beat.

Phil How do you feel, Frank?

Frank Okay . . .

Phil Did you have a glance at those mags . . . ?

Frank Oh yeah . . . very nice, very tasteful . . . yeah . . .

Phil Educational, aren't they?

Frank Yeah . . .

Phil I've got a couple of videos that might be worth a nod . . .

Frank Oh, right . . . tomorrow night, maybe . . . after the game?

Phil Let's see how it goes . . .

Tony How do you think we'll do?

Phil Dunno . . .

Frank I must admit that I think we look quite good . . .

Tony Depends who Arthur's bringing in . . .

Phil I've got a feeling that that might be another of Arthur's little foibles . . .

Frank Yeah . . . you might be right . . .

Tony Oh . . . If we lose, he's knackered.

Phil That's the price of gambling . . .

Tony Funny how you just do things, don't you . . . ? Make a decision to do something and then do it . . . That marathon . . . they do it just to say they've done it.

Phil Creativity, isn't it?

Tony Is it?

Phil Well, what would you have been doing if you hadn't been training . . . ?

Tony   Arsing about, I suppose.

Phil   Right . . . it's all part of the creative impulse . . . I tell the kids at school . . . creativity takes on many forms . . . They can't see it.

Frank   Well, it's part of the health thing, isn't it . . . ? Life's like a tightrope . . . I read this in a book somewhere . . . never really forgotten it . . . life's a tightrope . . . we all travel in one direction, and if we don't surround ourselves with things to do . . . to help balance us . . . we fall off . . . something like that, anyway . . .

Phil   I think I know what you mean.

Tony   Do you think we ought to help Arthur out if we lose?

Frank   In what way?

Tony   With the money.

Phil   We're not going to lose . . . no way am I having a woman make my back and legs and arms ache for five weeks to lose . . . no way . . . Shower, Frank . . . ?

Frank   No . . .

Phil   Tony . . . ?

Tony   Can do . . .

Phil   See you there . . .

Tony   See you . . .

Hazel *enters, carrying fresh towels.*

Phil   See you tomorrow, Hazel . . . You'll be there, won't you?

Hazel   Oh don't worry . . . I wouldn't miss it for the world . . .

Phil
Tony } (*together*)   See you.

Tony and **Phil** exit.

Hazel Aren't you going for a drink, Frank?

Frank No . . .

Hazel Oh . . .

Frank I don't feel like it, to be honest . . .

Hazel That's a shame . . .

Frank I feel all melancholy.

Hazel Oh, what's brought that on?

Frank This game.

Hazel Oh . . .

Frank When I was younger I used to play regularly . . .
Tina would bring the kids to watch . . .

Hazel Aren't they coming tomorrow . . . ?

Frank No . . .

Hazel Oh . . .

Frank We . . . er . . . we split up, you see . . .

Hazel Oh, I'm sorry . . .

Frank Took the kids . . . I hardly see them now. They
used to love to come and watch . . . Carl and Peter . . . two
good props in the making . . . Their mother'll be making
them as soft as pudding.

Hazel That's mothers for you.

Frank Do you have any kids . . . ?

Hazel No . . .

Frank All this serious training, the lads as a team . . .
brought it all back to me . . .

Hazel Yeah?

Frank I wasn't bothered when we were losing . . . it didn't matter then, but we're in with a chance now . . . I want them to be proud of me, do you know that . . . ? I want them to be proud of me . . . and she's making them as soft as shit . . .

Hazel Go home, Frank . . .

Frank Yeah . . .

Hazel Save all the hatred for the field.

Frank You know what, Hazel?

Hazel No, what?

Frank Well, the lads and me were talking and we think that you're all right for a woman . . .

Hazel Well that's very big of 'em, Frank . . . very big of 'em . . .

Frank I think that I will have that drink after all. Are you coming?

A beat.

Hazel Well if I'm going to be one of the lads, I think I'd better.

They exit.

The lights cover to blue wash. All the gym equipment is removed save the two benches, which are placed side by side mid-stage. Brass music.

Arthur *enters and stands centre stage.*

Hazel *is downstage in a spotlight.*

Hazel So a steady drink for one and all, and then home to bed as the hour moved on apace. Our heroes bid each other adieu, and with confidence in their hearts they knew they stood a chance, a chance to win, to regain lost pride. They knew that fate was on their side.

Arthur   I know it sounds funny but that night I prayed, I don't know why, I'm agnostic. Then I looked at my bankbook, placed it under Doreen's underwear in the bottom drawer, then I went to sleep.

The lights fade on **Arthur** *who exits.*

Phil *enters, with a hot-water bottle, wearing a dressing-gown.*

Hazel   Though Arthur slept in slumberland, in Phil's three-bedroomed semi his mind was filled with nightmarish thoughts and sleep he hadn't any.

The spot goes out on **Hazel***, who exits.*

Phil   It's a very funny thing, when I was playing at Loughborough I never got nervous, I never had a thought about the game but tonight I'm like a bag of nerves . . . I've been to the toilet . . . back here to bed . . . I'm going to the toilet again in a minute . . . I'm sweating, sweat's dripping down my brow, even my palms are wet . . . I'll have to hope that I can, well . . . drift off to sleep.

The lights change to a red wash covering the stage.

And there I was, playing at Wembley in the Challenge Cup Final, playing for Fulham against the mighty Featherstone . . . There was hundreds and hundreds of bloated red faces looking down on me . . . I was on the wing and hundreds of yards away from the rest of the team. Featherstone looked massive . . . I gazed up and caught flashes of their kneecaps . . . They ran through to score, I glimpsed sight of hairs on the palms of their hands. We were losing . . . We needed a try. There was five minutes to play . . . There was an incident off the ball . . . 'Gerroff me, you fat pig.' I saw a gap, big as an ocean opening up in front of me . . . 'Pass the ball . . . pass the ball!' And then it came out of a blur, the ball . . . God, I was nervous . . . I saw it coming towards me . . . daren't take my eye off it . . . I caught it and I ran . . . But I didn't move . . . I looked up . . . and the whole of Featherstone were coming towards me . . . men, women, children . . . miners, shop assistants, garage-owners . . . all

on the field after me . . . so I ran . . . but the faster I ran the
slower I went . . . I looked around for someone to pass to . . .
but they were all having lunch . . . sat down having lunch
in the middle of Wembley Stadium . . . 'Go on, Phil,' they
said, 'Go on . . . run mate, run' . . . and I was on the
underground going down the Piccadilly Station, running
and they were all running after me . . . Then a policeman
stopped me and I tried to explain but he wanted my name
and where I lived . . . I hit him . . . and ran . . . It was like
running in a dream . . . jumping over buildings and landing
at different places . . . but wherever I landed they were still
there, coming around the corner . . . I ran up an alleyway
. . . I was cornered . . . I looked around at them . . . trapped,
so I ran towards them . . . I just closed my eyes and ran . . .

Phil *exits.*

A bluish-coloured wash covers the stage, quite dimly.

Arthur, **Tony**, **Frank** *and* **Steve** *move about in the lights,
growling and making large movements. They are the Cobblers team.
They arrange the benches so they're like they were at the beginning of
Act One. The players sit down. On the backs of their shirts they have
'Cobblers Arms' emblazoned. They wear full rugby regalia – the
players will play the parts of both teams. The lights come up.*

Arthur   Somebody's gonna get smacked . . .

Tony   Yeah . . .

Frank   I'm gonna kill somebody.

Tony   Yeah, kill!

Steve   Hurt their bodies . . .

Arthur   Somebody's gonna get their neck broke and their
body hurt.

Tony   Yeah . . . and hurt . . .

Frank   What are we?

All   Mean.

Frank   What do we want?

All   We want to win.

Frank   What will we do?

All   We'll kill to win.

Frank   Who are we gonna kill?

All   The Wheatsheaf wallies.

Frank   Why?

All   'Cos we hate the bastards . . .

Arthur (*shaking his fist*)   Somebody's gonna get some of this . . . !

Tony   Keep the ball tight . . . until we've made the overlap . . .

Steve   Don't switch it, then . . .

Arthur   Run straight at 'em . . . Run till you can see the whites of their eyes, and when you can see the whites . . . stick an arm straight in 'em . . .

Frank   Right, here we go . . .

Arthur   Put the willies up 'em . . .

They sing a war-like chant, with a slapping of thighs and a banging of feet on the floor. This gets louder and louder, ending in screams and growls.

Blackout.

The lights come up to reveal the same players, but very quiet (in total contrast) and sitting down. They have just heard what the Cobblers have done.

Steve   Hear that?

Tony   Yeah.

Steve   Jesus Christ, I'm shitting it . . .

Arthur   Ar . . .

Frank   I think they mean business . . .

Tony   Do they know that we've had a bye on purpose?

Arthur   Yeah . . .

Tony   They are not going to be too happy about that, are they?

Arthur   No . . .

Steve   Have they got seven men . . . ?

Frank   And two subs . . . I watched them play the first round.

Tony   Yeah, the subs are like whippets . . .

Steve   They would be . . .

Arthur   Remember what I've said all along . . . don't let your nerves get the better of you. Stick to the plans . . .

Tony   Where's Phil . . . ?

Phil *enters, walking as if he's got the shits – which he has.*

Phil   Have you seen the size of that lot?

Steve   Where've you been, man . . . ?

Phil   Toilet . . .

Tony   Trying to escape . . .

Phil   I'm loose.

Frank   We'll all be loose by the time we've finished this . . .

Phil   They have got some big lads.

Arthur   Yeah . . . and they've brought a couple of ringers in.

Tony   He wants his money, doesn't he?

Arthur   He's not gonna get it, though . . . over my dead body . . .

Steve   Hey, steady on, Arthur, I'll play but I'm not going that far.

Tony   How long is there?

Arthur   Five minutes . . .

Frank   Let them go out first . . .

Phil   They're out . . . I could hear them changing when I was on the toilet . . . the seat was vibrating.

Steve   What's the weather like . . . ?

Phil   Not bad . . . good for running.

Arthur   Keep it wide . . . don't let them keep it tight . . .

Tony   Wide . . . right . . .

Steve   Oh, before I forget, Arthur . . . nice one on the kit . . .

Frank   Oh yeah . . . good stuff, mate.

Tony   Yeah . . .

Arthur   I know this is the wrong time to say this, lads . . . but I had to fork out a fiver each for the hire of the kit . . . if at some time in the not too distant future . . .

Phil   Did I have a dream last night?

Steve   And me . . . I was playing at Wembley.

Phil *looks at him.*

Frank   I know what you mean, I was playing all last night.

Arthur   Remember the set moves when you get a call . . . move it, right?

All   Right.

Steve   Arthur, I suppose these ringers you were talking about were just figments of your imagination, they're not going to appear, are they?

A beat.

Arthur   Ar well . . . it's a very long and complicated story.

A beat.

All   Ay, it would be.

Hazel *enters, wearing the same kit. Music plays.*

All the players look together as a team at **Arthur**.

Steve   You're not serious?

Frank   Is this the arrangement? I mean, she might get hurt.

Hazel   Well, what did you expect?

Phil   Does she know the moves? I mean, I'm not being rotten, Hazel, just . . . well you know?

Arthur   Where do you think I got the idea from?

Frank   He is not thick.

Steve   No, we are.

Tony   Well, if you play as good as you train . . . it's okay by me . . .

Steve   And me.

Phil   And me.

Hazel   Right, thanks team . . .

Tony   I feel a bit emotional . . .

Frank   Let's get out there . . .

Arthur   Yeah . . .

Tony   Having a woman playing . . . I love it, aarrhhh!

Phil   It will probably throw 'em.

Steve   It's thrown me.

Arthur   Well, let's just say . . . all the best . . .

Frank   All the best, Arth . . .

Tony   Good luck.

Arthur   And you.

Phil   It's a ridiculous thing to do, Arthur . . . but thanks . . .

Hazel   If you don't live life to the full, what's the point?

Phil   Here we go, then . . .

They all prepare. There is a sudden air of complete seriousness. They shake and concentrate . . . and then . . . out into the stage space they run . . . They jump up and down in the stage space . . . **Arthur** *steps forward . . . and shakes hands with* '**Frank**' *of the Cobblers.*

Arthur   Hope it'll be a good game.

'**Frank**'   You're going to die.

Arthur   Don't be like that.

'**Frank**'   You're in a box.

Hazel   Which way are we playing, Arthur?

Arthur   Our kick-off.

Tony   What's their captain like?

Arthur   I think he must have trouble at home.

Steve   How come?

Arthur   He's not a happy man.

Phil   Oh . . .

Arthur   I don't think that they like us very much . . .

Steve   Funny, that . . . they look a friendly bunch . . .

Tony   Has anybody seen *Flesh-eating Zombies*?

Frank   I know what you're saying . . .

Phil   I don't like the look of mine . . .

Arthur   Man for man marking . . .

Tony   I'll have yours, then . . .

Phil   Right, fill out the space . . . all the area . . .

The players move into the space.

Steve   They are massive . . .

Phil   I bet they can't run . . .

Steve   Half of 'em can't talk . . . (*He mimics a gross beast.*)

Hazel   They've got legs like tree-trunks and shoulders like they'd swallowed two dustbins . . . They hate us . . . you can see it . . .

Frank   Why do the opposition always look so big?

Tony   I bet they've only got four teeth between 'em . . .

Phil   Watch for the funny switch . . . up on 'em quick . . .

Tony   Once the first tackle's been made I'll be okay . . .

Steve   I'm like a jellyfish . . .

Hazel   How do you think I feel?

A beat.

Frank   Straight on 'em, a man each . . .

Arthur   Anybody ever seen *Zulu*?

Tony   He's off . . .

Steve   You ought to be on 'Film Eighty-Four'.

Arthur   It reminds me of *Zulu* . . . Rourke's Drift . . . we're the British . . . they're the . . .

Phil   Warriors . . . millions of 'em, all stood on the cliffs, I've seen it . . .

Frank   Looks like it . . . and all . . .

Phil   Yeah . . . they all got killed . . .

Arthur   They got VCs though . . .

Tony   I'll be Michael Caine . . .

Steve   Aren't we having a team photo, Arthur . . .

Arthur   We'll have it later . . .

Steve   In hospital?

A whistle is blown.

Hazel   Arthur kicked off a large rambling grubber kick
along the ground . . . The sound of leather on leather was
sickening, even from the kick-off . . .

Tony   Nobbler Knowles . . .

Phil   For the Cobblers caught the ball . . .

Steve   Their most feared forward . . .

Arthur *during this time has held off a ball.* **Frank** *positions himself
so that the back of his shirt shows the Cobbler's insignia – he is
therefore now Nobbler Knowles.* **'Frank'** *takes the ball at pace, and
despite desperate tackles from the Wheatsheaf players he scores a try
downstage-centre. He turns round and becomes* **Frank** *again.
Dejection amongst the Wheatsheaf side. They retrieve the ball.*

Phil   Steve . . . tackle!

Steve   Tackle that?

Phil   Yeah . . .

Steve   I didn't see you making much effort . . .

Phil   I was covering . . .

Steve   I was covering . . .

Tony   Your eyes, eh?

Hazel   Good start, lads . . .

Frank   What about the conversion . . . ?

Phil   They'll not bother . . . They know that they've won.

Arthur   Right, come on . . . let's see nobody chickening out, right?

Arthur, **Hazel**, **Phil** *and* **Steve** *move sideways across the stage, covering the Cobblers.*

Our kick . . .

Hazel   Arthur kicked a nice long one, which bounced inside their twenty-two metres line . . .

Steve   For God's sake, watch that big un . . .

Arthur *passes the ball to* '**Frank**' *(Nobbler), who runs and is challenged by* **Steve** *and* **Phil**, *but manages to pass to* '**Tony**' *(Stabber), who tries to get around* **Arthur** *and does, but is caught by the shirt by* **Hazel**. *She tries to push him back, but he runs to score another try for the Cobblers.*

Hazel   Sorry, lads . . . I had him . . .

Tony   Eight–nil . . . in two minutes . . .

Steve   It's all over, lads . . .

Tony   You said it . . .

Steve   All over . . .

Tony   Oh shite . . .

Arthur   Come on . . . get it together . . . they're only flesh and blood . . . Think about the game . . . Come on! . . . ! (*Shouting.*) Long kick, Phil . . . (*Whispering.*) Short one . . .

'**Tony**'   Watch out for the long one . . .

Arthur *rolls the ball on-stage.* **Phil** *runs forward and picks up the ball.* '**Tony**' *(Stabber) is over him and won't let him play the ball.*

Play the ball . . .

Phil   In a tick . . .

'Tony'   Play the ball . . .

Phil   Let me get up, then . . .

'Tony'   Play the ball . . . !

Phil   Hang on . . .

'Tony'   Play it . . . !

Phil   All right . . . no need to get physical . . .

A push from **'Tony'**.

Steady on . . . it's only a game . . .

'Tony'   Come on then, short-arse . . .

Another push from **'Tony'**.

Phil   Look, will you pack that in?

Steve   Send him to the back of the class, Phil . . .

'Tony'   Play the ball . . .

Phil *plays the ball to* **Hazel**, *who passes to* **Arthur**, *who passes to* **Steve**. **Steve** *is hit by* **'Frank'** *(Nobbler) in the goolies and falls in agony to the floor. He writhes for a while.*

Steve   Oh . . . !

Phil   Come on, Steve, play the ball . . .

'Frank'   Play the ball . . .

Steve   Oh . . . oh . . . oh . . . my goolies . . . I'm ruined . . . I'm finished . . .

'Frank'   Play the ball . . .

Arthur   Count 'em . . .

Phil   He's only got one . . .

Hazel   Fourth tackle coming up . . .

Steve *gets up.* **Tony** *comes to watch him.* **'Frank'** *becomes*
Frank. **Steve** *plays the ball to* **Hazel** *who plays a blind-side ball*
to **Frank**, *who takes it and growls his way to centre stage.*

Hazel   Go on, Frank.

Steve   Leg it, Frankie . . .

Frank *begins to move but is brought down by* **'Tony'** *(Stabber).*
'Tony' *stands over* **Frank** *in the same manner as before.*

'Tony'   Play the ball . . .

Frank   Hang on a minute, man . . .

'Tony'   Play the ball . . . !

Frank   Hang on . . .

'Tony'   Play it . . . !

In slow motion **Frank** *grabs* **'Tony'** *by the shirt, brings his head*
back and nuts him full in the face. The reaction is given from the rest of
the players who make the sound effects. **'Tony'** *goes down and*
bounces off the floor.

Phil   Nice, Frank . . .

Frank *(to the referee)*   I think he's got something in his eye,
ref.

Frank *plays the ball to* **Hazel**, *to* **Arthur**, *to* **Steve** *(who is*
struggling after the kick in the goolies).

Steve   Not to me . . . I can't move . . . (**Steve** *passes the ball*
to **Phil**.)

Phil   I found some space on the left, even if it meant
running around the back of our line . . . I put my head down
and ran . . .

Arthur   Go on, Phil . . .

Hazel   Nice, Phil . . .

Frank   Lovely man . . . go on, yer . . .

Phil   A man to beat . . .

'Tony' *tackles but* **Phil** *breaks free. He scores in the corner. He and the rest of the team are elated.*

A try . . . a try in the corner . . . !

Steve   I don't believe it . . .

Tony   Whooh . . . !

Shouts of delight all round.

Frank   Brilliant . . . !

Arthur   Great solo effort, lads . . . great solo effort . . . well played lads.

Phil (*breathless*)   Thanks . . .

Hazel   Eight–four . . .

Arthur   Come on, we can beat these . . .

Hazel   One flukey try . . .

Arthur   We can hammer this lot . . .

Phil   Hey, look at 'em, they don't believe it . . .

Phil *makes a 'V' sign at the audience.*

Tony   Come on, keep it going . . .

Hazel *stands centre stage. The rest of the players are at the back of the stage.* **Hazel** *picks up the ball. The rest prepare to work a move.*

Hazel   You could see that they didn't like it . . . It was eight–four, with three minutes of the first half left to play. Their kick to us a long one right down to the touch in goal area . . . I picked it up and they were on us like growling bears . . .

Steve   Hazel . . . !

Hazel   I saw Steve coming inside, calling out . . .

Steve   Here . . . give it . . .

Steve receives the ball and begins to run downstage left. **Tony** *comes from upstage left and takes the ball on a scissor movement.* **Tony** *has the ball* C *and delivers a reverse pass to* **Phil**, *who gives a quick ball to* **Frank**, *who finds* **Arthur**. **Arthur** *takes the ball on downstage and performs a dummy downstage right, and moves centre stage. (This movement must be done at speed in order to get the slow-motion effect later.)* **Arthur** *stands centre.*

Arthur   And I'm there in the clear with about ten yards to go . . . and there it is, another try . . . beneath the sticks a captain's try . . . yes, what a marvellous equalising try from Billy Boston.

Arthur *dives. The players celebrate and lift* **Arthur** *aloft.*

Tony   Half-time.

Phil   Eight–all.

All   Eight all eight all eight all eight all.

Arthur *drops his shorts, baring his bum to the Cobblers.*

Steve   Up yours, Reg Welsh.

A change of colour wash to blue for voice-over action replay.

Voice-over (*in an Eddie Waring accent*)   Now let's just have a look at that try once again . . . let's see how it all started, Alex . . . Cobblers kick long and it's collected by Scott . . . formerly of Hunslett . . . and moved swiftly . . . out to Steve Edwards, who's a little slow for a big fellow really, Alex . . . to Burtoft who does well, and then this man Hopley, formerly of London . . . and the England Colts . . . and a fine runner with the ball to Rowley, looking tired and drawn . . . and a captain's try, Alex, for Arthur Hoyle, formerly of Wakefield . . . so as we go into the break it's even stevens . . .

Throughout the recent commentary the players have been re-running the whole of the last try sequence. (If the players are of a standard and the space permits, then sundry other moves can well be improvised.) At the completion of the re-run the players sit down, breathless, in the middle of the field. It is indeed half-time.

Steve   Eight–all . . .

Phil   It would have been ten–eight if we'd have bothered with the conversion . . .

Tony   Forget that . . . we can score tries . . . just keep the ball away from them big 'uns . . .

Steve   Anybody got any beer?

Frank   I've got a feeling that they're gonna get nasty this next half . . .

Phil   Yeah, watch that number eight . . .

Frank   I'll have him . . .

Hazel   Poke his eyes out . . . he scratched me . . .

Arthur   Hazel . . . you're doing well . . .

Tony   Yeah . . . not bad . . .

Phil   They're trying to keep it tight . . .

Arthur   Keep tackling up, man and ball . . . I think we've thrown 'em . . .

Phil   We're doing all right . . .

Steve   We're doing brilliant . . .

Arthur   Keep it on this half these ten minutes . . . think about it . . . when you go in go in and mean it . . . look for the blind side moves . . . let's see some flair . . . see some ball play . . .

Tony   I'll tell you what . . . the crowd are loving this . . . I can hear Gayle shouting a mile away . . .

Steve   Can I have my share of the brass now Arth?

Arthur   Don't speak too soon . . .

Phil   Look at 'em . . . bringing two subs on . . . ringers . . .

Arthur   Bastards . . .

Frank   Do you know 'em?

Arthur   One of them was a Warrington winger . . .

Tony   Wonder what they're saying . . .

Blackout. Gruff, fierce voices of the Cobblers team are heard.

'Frank'   Get that bald head and smash it . . .

'Arthur'   Yeah . . .

'Phil'   Throw the ball about to the wings more . . .

'Steve'   Try and stretch 'em . . .

'Frank'   Yeah, stretch 'em . . .

'Tony'   Start putting it together . . . They've come at us . . . Let's start getting back at them . . .

'Arthur'   Above all make every tackle hurt . . . Let them know that they've been in a game.

'Frank'   And hurt 'em . . .

The lights come back up on the Wheatsheaf team.

Phil   Right, we're ready . . .

Arthur   Hey, I've just had a thought . . .

Frank   What?

Arthur   Wait here . . . shan't be a minute . . .

Arthur *exits.*

Steve   Where's he going?

Tony   Probably had a brain-wave . . .

Hazel   I've got a feeling that this is going to be a long ten minutes . . .

Phil   Listen, Hazel, when you get a break, when you see a gap, go for it . . . you're being predictable.

Hazel   Right . . .

Arthur *returns with six gum-shields.*

Arthur   Here . . . wear these . . . I'd forgotten about 'em
. . . If it's going to get rough . . . it might save a few teeth for
someone . . .

*They all fit their gum-shields. All the players go out on to the pitch.
They attempt to talk to each other, but no one can understand what the
others are saying. In response to every remark there is a
misunderstanding nod. The image should be funny . . . until . . .*

Steve   I'm not wearing this, Arthur . . .

Frank   Nor me . . .

Arthur   Stick it down your sock in that case . . .

Some stick it down their socks. Some merely throw them to the side.

So at eight–all we had a chance . . .

Phil   But the Cobblers were no duck eggs . . .

Frank   They came back at us with open rugby . . .

Steve   And by one minute into the second half . . .

Tony   They had scored two remarkable tries . . .

Frank   Which they converted . . .

Hazel   The score was twenty points to eight . . .

Arthur   We started to swing the ball about . . .

Frank   Gave it some air . . .

Tony   Every opening we saw we went for with close
support . . .

Phil   With overlaps . . . and quick switching of the ball . . .

Steve   Tony scored . . . under the posts . . .

Hazel   Arthur converted and the score was
twenty–fourteen . . .

Arthur   Scrum down . . .

The front row is down. **Hazel** *has the ball. They prepare to go into the scrum position. As they go down there is much growling and biting of ears.*

Frank   Come here, I'll bite your neck off . . .

Hazel *puts the ball into the scrummage.* **Arthur** *hooks.* **Hazel** *takes the ball and works a scissors with* **Phil**, *who runs into the front row. He is brought down with a sickening thud. He gets up and pushes the tackler in the chest. There ensues a series of pushing involving all the players. The word they use is 'Yeah': hence 'Yeah', 'Yeah', 'Come on', 'Yeah', until a rather nasty scene of fighting breaks out.* **Arthur** *has eventually to be held back by the rest of the players as he threatens the audience.*

Arthur   Right, hit me . . . just hit me, let's see what that'll prove . . . yeah, you chickens . . . I'd take you all on . . . all of you.

Phil   Leave it, Arthur . . .

Arthur   Don't like it, do you? . . . Come on, play the ball, we've got these . . .

Tony   I got the ball inside their twenty-two . . .

Hazel   And quick as a flash . . .

Frank   Tony had scored a drop-kick . . .

They all cheer.

Steve   One point for that . . . pathetic rules . . .

Hazel   Twenty points to fifteen . . .

Arthur   How long left, ref?

Phil   Two minutes . . .

Frank   Don't let them in our half . . .

Steve   For those two minutes the Cobblers threw everything they had at us . . . It was man to man tackling all the way, now.

Three players are the Cobblers and three the Wheatsheaf. Throughout this it's a tackle on a man each. As they pass the ball from player to player **Steve** *intercepts and waves the ball at the audience.*

Steve I got the ball from a Cobbler's mistake . . .

Steve *gets the ball and weaves in and out of the rest of the players.* **Hazel** *stays upstage and* **Steve** *passes the ball to her. The rest of the team stand* DR *in pairs ready to catch* **Steve**. **Steve** *gives and gets the ball from* **Hazel**. *He runs towards the three Cobblers players and jumps into their arms. He makes two attempts to play the ball over the line. On the third he succeeds, and is held aloft by the three, who are now the Wheatsheaf team. Exaltation abounds.*

A try . . . a try . . . right in the corner . . .

Phil Why didn't you go under the sticks?

Steve A try . . . in the corner . . .

They all congratulate **Steve**.

Tony It was a long kick . . . I took it . . . but the angle was too acute . . .

Tony *mimes the ball going towards the posts. In the event it misses, and the players illustrate their dismay.*

Bastard . . . sorry, lads . . .

Hazel Twenty–nineteen.

Arthur One minute left.

Frank Watch the time-wasting, ref.

Phil Watch the kick . . .

The players are all standing upstage, **Frank** *has the ball behind his back. The line-up across the stage reads:* **Frank**, **Phil**, **Arthur**, **Tony**, **Steve**, **Hazel**.

Steve As soon as you get it, attack . . .

Arthur Fifty seconds . . .

Tony Get it kicked, man . . . Ref, that's time-wasting . . .

Arthur   They kicked . . . it was long . . . but I expected that . . .

Frank *tosses the ball from behind his back to* **Phil** *during the next sequence of dialogue. The ball goes all the way down the line to* **Hazel***, who passes back inside to* **Steve***.* **Phil** *has dropped backstage.* **Tony***,* **Arthur** *and* **Frank** *have become the Cobblers centre stage.*

Phil   I stayed back and set off on a long run . . .

Frank   Close support was needed . . .

Steve   Up and under . . . !

Steve *has the ball. He hoists the ball with a boot.* **Hazel** *takes it from behind his back.* **Phil** *runs and is hoisted into the air by Cobblers. (*'**Frank**'*,* '**Tony**' *and* '**Arthur**'*).* **Hazel** *tosses the ball to* **Phil** *and* '**Frank**' *(Nobbler) hits him in the mouth. They all fall to the ground.* **Hazel** *blows the whistle. All are on the floor.* **Phil** *holds his mouth.*

All   Penalty, ref . . . !

Steve   I'll take it.

Hazel   Let me take it.

Tony   I'll take it.

Frank   Let Phil take it . . .

Steve   Let Tony have a go . . .

Arthur   I'll take it . . .

Frank   Don't miss . . .

Hazel   Twenty seconds left . . . This would be the last kick of the game . . .

Arthur   I could kick this in my slippers . . .

Phil   Take your time . . .

Tony   Don't hook it . . .

Arthur   I know it's a straight-forward kick . . .

Hazel   Arthur carefully placed the ball . . .

Tony   Considered its oval shape . . .

Phil   Wiped the mud from his boot . . .

Steve   Stood slowly upright . . .

Frank   Stepped back majestically . . .

Phil   Raised his head . . .

Steve   And struck the ball beautifully . . .

Hazel   We looked up to see the ball soar . . . into the air . . .

Phil   High, very high . . .

Steve   We watched the ball . . .

Tony   As it . . . ?

Arthur   Struck the post . . .

Frank   And bounced back towards us . . .

All the players mouth 'Fucking hell' as they see defeat. A whistle is blown.

Tony   Full time.

Arthur   Shit . . . shit . . . shit . . .

Arthur *falls to the floor: 'Jesus Christ'. The other players are stunned. There is a moment's silence.*

Don't anybody talk to me.

Tony   What're you going to do, Arthur?

Arthur   Kill myself . . .

The rest of the team sit about.

Phil   I'm off . . .

Tony   Where?

Phil   Get changed.

Both go and stand upstage centre, with their backs to the audience, holding hands as the Cobblers.

Steve   Whoooh, eh? Twenty-bloody-nineteen . . .

Frank   We had 'em worried, though . . .

'Phil' }
'Tony' }   (*together*)   Well played, Cobblers.

Steve *and* **Frank** *get a bench each and sit on it. The lights fade to interior.*

Hazel   I didn't know what to do or what to say . . . They seemed to have nothing left . . . nothing left to give . . . We all crept silently back to the dressing-room and sat . . .

Arthur *is still left on-stage, crying, but the location has changed to the dressing-room. The players sit and remain silent for a long, long time. They begin to take off their shoes, socks, shirts, etc.*

Tony   Rocky didn't cry, Arthur . . .

Arthur   I know . . .

Tony   Yeah . . .

Arthur   *Rocky*'s a bleeding film . . .

Tony   I know . . .

Frank   Oh, well . . .

A number of cans of beer are intermittently pulled open.

Steve   Well, we can't all be Rocky Balboa, but . . . ?

Phil   At least we tried . . .

Frank   'Pack up all my cares and woe . . . here I go, singing low . . .'

Arthur   We didn't finish the marathon, though, did we . . . ?

Frank   'Bye bye blackbird . . .'

Arthur   Sorry, lads . . . I've let you down . . .

Steve   Don't worry, Arthur . . . we'll beat 'em next time . . .

Arthur   You what?

Frank   'Where somebody waits for me . . .'

Steve   Next time we play 'em . . . the bastards, I got a right crack on my ear . . .

Frank   'Sugar's sweet, so is she . . .'

Arthur   No . . . there's no next time . . .

Frank   'Bye bye blackbird . . .'

Tony   What about the five weeks' trial . . . ?

Phil   Yeah, you've passed . . . coach for life . . .

Hazel   Another challenge, Arthur . . .

Arthur   No . . .

Phil   Listen you stay with us . . . you and us lot . . . we're a good team . . .

Frank   'No one here can love or understand me, oh what hard-luck stories they all hand me . . .'

Phil   A great team.

Steve   One lousy point . . .

Frank   There's worse things happen in the world . . .

Arthur   As my dad always said, there's always another day . . .

Phil   Very true . . .

Arthur   I suppose that . . . oh no . . .

Frank   Go on . . .

Steve   Suppose what?

Arthur   I've got this daft idea that we go over to Reg Welsh . . . right . . . ? Double or nothing . . .

Phil   And they field no ringers?

Arthur   Exactly . . .

Tony   That's six grand . . . Shit . . . This could go on for ever . . .

Frank   But next time we'll win . . .

Steve   I'm in for that . . . Let's show these bastards . . .

Phil   I thought this was your last game?

Steve   It was . . .

Frank   Just one point . . .

Arthur   What?

Frank   We find a kicker . . .

Hazel   I can goal kick . . .

Tony   Why didn't you say owt?

Hazel   Nobody asked me . . .

Arthur   So . . .

Steve   So what?

Arthur   Is it on . . . ?

Steve
Hazel } (*together*)   You bet . . .
I'm in.

Tony
Phil } (*together*)   It's on . . .
Let's kill 'em . . .

Arthur   What if Reg won't accept the bet?

All   Oh yeah . . .

Frank *begins to sing once more. Slowly they all begin to join in the song of 'Bye bye blackbird'.* **Arthur** *is the last one to join in. As they reach the end of the second verse they are transformed.* Rocky *theme* *music plays, and slowly they all stand. Each character is introduced over a loudspeaker and the name of the actor given, like at the end of Dallas-style soap opera. As the credits are given the actors play selected parts of the play:* **Tony***'s try,* **Steve***'s try,* **Hazel***'s exercises,* **Frank***'s head butt.* **Phil** *is the last one, with a smack in the mouth. All the players raise a hand to the audience, give a knowing smile that 'Up 'n' Under Two' is coming and take their bows . . .*

April in Paris

To Jane

April in Paris was first performed on 23 April 1992 at the Spring Street Theatre, Hull, by the Hull Truck Theatre Company as part of the Hull 1992 Festival.

Al   John Godber
Bet   Jane Clifford

Directed by John Godber
Designed by Rob Jones
Director's Assistant Zoe Seaton

The action takes place in a space representing several locations.

Time – the 1990s.

Act One

Playover: Edith Piaf Collection.

A space. In the middle of the space is a white box (a white floor and white flats about ten feet square). Two white chairs fill the box. A hanging light (practical) is visible.

Introduction music plays, a laconic French tune. The house lights fade. **Bet** *enters. She is wearing black and white. She sits on a chair and reads a copy of* Bella *magazine.*

The lights face. **Al** *enters. He is a large, distraught man in his late thirties, also wearing black and white. Music fades.*

Al   Are you back?

Bet   No.

Al   Oh.

Bet   Yeah.

Al   Oh.

Bet   Yeah.

Al   Do you want a coffee making?

Bet   No.

Al   Are you sure?

Bet   Yeah.

Al   Oh.

Bet   Been int shed?

Al   Yeah.

Bet   Oh . . .

Al   All day . . .

Bet   Ah . . .

Al   Yeah.

Bet   How's it going?

Al   All rate.

Bet   Nowt ont telly.

Al   No.

Bet   Cold in here.

Al   Heating's on.

Bet   Is it?

Al   Yeh.

Bet (*looking at the magazine*)   Oh, this looks good.

Al   Shall I make a pot of tea?

Bet   I'm not bothered.

Al   I'll leave it then.

Bet (*looking at the magazine*)   Oh yes, this looks good.

Al   What is it?

Bet   A competition.

Al   Oh.

Bet   Well . . .

Al   Don't enter another competition.

Bet   Why not?

Al   It's embarrassing.

Bet   It is not.

Al   What are you trying to win?

Bet   A life.

Al   A life . . .

Bet   Somewhere away from you . . .

Al   Oh . . .

Bet   Somewhere nice . . .

Al   I'll help you do it if you want.

Bet   You've no need.

Al   What do you win?

Bet   I'm not telling you.

Al   It's full of rubbish anyway . . .

Silence. **Bet** *sits and reads* Bella.

Bet (*reading the magazine*)   Oh this is interesting. It says here that according to a survey most Yorkshire men would prefer a pint than making love with their wives.

Pause.

Al   What sort of pint?

Bet   It says twenty per cent would rather go to the pub.

Al   If they've got any money.

Bet   And that fifty-one per cent would rather pursue a hobby, that's you. Oh, they watch twenty-one hours telly a week – I wonder if that includes videos – and listen to twelve hours music, well, that's not you – you hate music, don't you?

Al   At least I don't read rubbish.

Bet   It's not rubbish.

Al   At least I read sommat decent.

Bet   'S boring what you read. Just a load of pictures.

Pause.

Al   Many in town?

Bet   Empty.

Al   No money about.

Bet I tret myself to a little treat today. Sommat to wear.

Al What was it, a gas mask?

Bet You think you're funny.

Al I did once.

Bet A scarf. There's nobody shopping in town. There's tumbleweed blowing around the streets.

Al Better tell the Council, they should see to that.

Bet Bought myself a scarf. Saved up, made me feel a bit better, cheered me up a bit.

Al You should've got me one. I suit a scarf.

Bet Oh you.

Al What?

Bet You think you're so funny.

Silence. **Bet** *sees something in the magazine.*

Bet Hey, I think I can do this one.

Al You say that about them all.

Bet I know this one.

Al Don't enter another competition for God's sake.

Bet Shut up you.

Al It's all a fix. You've got more chance of flying to the moon.

Bet Don't be such a spoilsport.

Al You never win owt.

Bet I nearly won a Jaguar once. I only entered that for you. That thing in the supermarket, win a Jag, I entered that one for you.

Al You entered for yourself.

Bet   I can't drive.

Silence.

Al   You never win owt.

Bet   I won a cool bag . . . four golf balls . . . I won some dog food once . . .

Al   How's it going at work?

Bet   All rate . . .

Al   Ohhhhhh.

Silence.

Bet   Is it finished? That thing you're doing?

Al   It's not a thing I'm doing.

Bet   Go and get it, let's have a look.

Al   No. You're not interested.

Bet   Go on. Go on, let's have a look at it, it might be a masterpiece.

Al *gets up and slowly exits.*

(*Calling off after him.*) Go and bring it for me. Because if I don't see it you'll only have a tantrum and hit a door . . . or sommat . . .

Al *enters carrying a large canvas with an awful, monochromatic amateur painting of an industrial landscape on it. He is shy but proud.*

Al   I can hear you by the way, walls are paper thin.

Bet   I haven't said owt.

Al   Here you are.

Bet (*overreacting*)   Oh, oh, that's good, int it?

Al   Not bad is it?

Bet   It's like your others.

Al   I know. I try and paint sommat different but it always turns out like this.

Bet   And all them books you read about painting and all? No, it's good. It's great.

Al   It's not quite finished yet. I've got to sign it.

Bet   It looks finished to me. Completely finished.

Al   Don't be so funny.

Bet   Do you know it's lovely is that, and it'll come in handy.

Al   Can we hang it in the house?

Bet   It can go upstairs and stop that draught in the loo.

Al   Shall I take it back?

Al   If you want, don't ask me everything.

Al   I'll take it back, then, shall I?

He exits.

Bet (*calling after him*)   Rita at work asked if we wanted to go out with them. Her and Colin are going to that Over Twenty-Fives' Night in town.

Al *enters.*

She says it's a great laugh. She's asked me if we want to go. I said I'd ask you.

Al   What should I want to go for?

Bet   For a laugh, be all right, you'll get in, you're old enough.

Al   I'm not going, no point to it.

Bet   There is for a laugh, look on the bright side.

Al   There isn't a bright side. We've got six thousand to live on, now we can either pay the house off or be buried, take your pick.

Bet   Oh, don't start.

Al   And you're wanting to go to discos.

Bet   Well, you never do owt.

Al   Twenty years with that firm, building bloody boxes like this for people to sodding live in. A good wind would blow 'em over.

Bet   They're nice houses.

Al   Sat about in the back garden with the shirt off, showing off. And housewives bringing you tea and biscuits, treating you like gods. A god in their back garden. And they'd look at you and you'd know what they were thinking . . .

Bet   Well, I bet they weren't thinking it about you.

Al   I feel like a bloody leper now, I'm dropping to bits.

Bet   I wish you were still at work, I do.

Al   And kids nicking stuff off the site every night.

Bet   At least I didn't see that much of you . . .

Al   Why? And then we'd build 'em and the next thing you know they're covered in graffiti.

Bet   I'd forgotten what it was like spending nearly every waking hour with you.

Al   First four months, I thought it was great. No need to get up in a morning. Stay in bed all day, all night. And then it starts to get to you . . . You get up, light a fire, walk to the gate, come back, look at the fire. Go back to bed, might as well be dead.

Bet   I wish you were sometimes.

Al   I thought it would soon be over, but I was bloody wrong.

Bet   Go in the shed if you're going to shout.

Al   Sat in here all day . . .

Bet   I wish I could get my hands on whoever shut that firm. I'd bloody shoot 'em.

Al   This bloody house.

Bet   Just leave it.

Al   Where's the money going to come from? Every penny you get you spend.

Bet   That's not true.

Al   Bloody records, scarves, God knows what else.

Bet   I haven't bought any records for years.

Al   Bloody scarves.

Bet   It cost me four pounds, that's all.

Al   I'm redundant living in a bloody shed and you're swanning about buying scarves. Who do you think you are, Princess Anne?

Bet   I have a right to tret myself.

Al   You're buying scarves and we can't even go out for a drink.

Bet   You don't want to go out. We could go out and have a drink with Rita and Colin if you like. But you're too miserable, we could go out with them and have one drink.

Al   I'm not just having one drink. You go out with them if you want, but I'm not going out and sitting there all night with one drink.

Bet   No, I should've known. One drink's no good for you, is it?

Al   No, it's not.

Bet   You've got to have eight.

Al   You think you're funny. I could kill you sometimes, you right get under my skin.

Bet   And I could kill you and all, I could slit your throat and think I'd done nowt.

Al   Go on do it then.

Bet   I'll smash every painting in that bloody shed if you start.

Al   Go on then.

Bet   I could do better myself.

Al   Could you?

Bet   I could do better than you.

Al   Could you?

Bet   I could.

Al   You couldn't.

Bet   What do you do 'em for anyway, you won't let anybody see 'em, mind you, there's no wonder, I'd be ashamed.

Al   I do 'em for me. For me. Not for you, for me.

Bet   Yeah, typical, all for yourself.

Al   Shut up you and go and enter another competition. Hey, look at the time, it's ten to eight. You haven't entered a competition for an hour. Are you ill or sommat? I'll ring a doctor, shall I? It might be withdrawal symptoms. Hey I tell you what, I've seen one tonight. There's one in the paper, win a muzzle. Why don't you enter that?

Bet   You want a muzzle.

Al   Do I?

Bet   You do.

Al   I think I'll start entering, see if I can win a job.

Bet   Oh that was a joke? That's not like you to make a joke.

Al   It's the only way I'm gonna get one with this lot.

Bet   At least I can do 'em. I'm not like you. At least I know the bloody answers. You'd be no good, you don't know anything.

Al   That's true that is, you're right there.

Bet   You don't know anything.

Al   I don't know why I married you.

Bet   You think you're so funny, don't you?

Al   You make the answers up half the time.

Bet   I don't.

Al   How much do you spend on them bloody magazines?

Bet   That's got nowt to do with you, that, that's my pocket money, I do what I want with it.

Al   Oh shuddup.

You shuddup.

Blackout.

The lights come up. Days later. **Bet** *and* **Al** *change positions.*

Al   Do you want a coffee?

Bet   No.

Al   I'll make one . . .

Bet   I don't want one.

Al   Oh, right.

Bet   Thanks.

Al   I'll not have one then.

Bet   You can have one for me . . .

Al   It's not worth putting the kettle on for, is it?

Bet   You have one, I don't want one.

Al   Why don't you want one?

Bet   Why do you want one?

Al   Sommat to do.

Bet   I don't fancy a coffee, you have one. I'm not stopping you from having one.

Al   No point me having one, is there?

Pause.

Bet   There's nowt good ont telly tonight.

Al   We could watch the test card for a bit.

Bet   I've seen it.

Al *begins to prowl the white box.*

Al   This bloody house, I wish it'd blow up.

Bet   You don't.

Al   I wish the whole lot would blow up.

Bet   I wish you'd blow up. Pheeew bang, all over. Head all across the ceiling, bits of chest on the telly, stomach on the wall, limbs out of the window, floating about somewhere. I wish you'd blow up.

Al   I might go to bed.

Bet   Go then.

Al   I think I'll have a bath . . .

Bet   There's no water.

Al   What?

Bet   There's no hot water.

Al   Why?

Bet   I've had a bath.

Al   When?

Bet   When I came in from work. I had a soak because my feet were killing me so I had a soak.

Al   Oh right.

Bet   I had the water right up to the top and all. I had a right good soak.

Al   No bloody hot water now.

Al   Right up to the rim I had it.

Al   It should've drowned you.

Bet   It was nearly coming over, you should've seen me. And bubble bath, I had some of that green bubble bath, there was just a bit left so I had all suds. Ooh I looked like a bloody film star just laid there, soaking.

Al   Who do you think you are?

Bet   I love to soak.

Al   It ruins that bath.

Bet   It doesn't.

Al   It leaves a mark on the bath.

Bet   It doesn't.

Al   It does.

Bet   You're the one who leaves a mark around the bath.

Al   I do not.

Bet   You do, I don't tell you, but I clean up after you. Every time you get a bath there's a line of scum left around the bath. It's like your skin's peeling off. I have to get a cloth and scrape it off. I've done that and not told you for ten years.

Al   I'll start using bubble bath.

Bet   And you never stand on the bath mat. You leave these two great big sodden footprints on the carpet. You never do anything you're supposed to.

Al   I think I'll make myself a sandwich.

Bet   Another? You've had a dozen today.

Al   I've got to eat sommat, at least I'm not lounging about all day in the bloody bath.

Bet   You're only one grunt short of being a pig.

Al   Well, if I'm a pig what are you?

Bet   At least I like a laugh. You never want to do anything.

Al   I do.

Bet   I look at you sometimes and I wonder. We're only here once and look what I've ended up with.

Al   Why don't you leave then?

Bet   I might do.

Al   I've heard that before.

Bet   I did all sorts before I met you. I had a good life before I met you.

Al   Leave then. Go back to your dad, see if he wants you.

Bet   You're useless around the house. You can't cook. I have to do everything.

Al   Why do you stay then?

Bet   I don't know. Ten years.

Al   Nine.

Bet   Ten years in September. I wish I'd never said 'I do' sometimes.

Al   You silly woman.

Bet   Ten years and nothing to show for it except you.

Blackout.

The lights come up. Months later. Both are as they were earlier, but
Bet *is elated and jumping about.*

Bet   Ha ha, you're wrong aren't you, admit it, admit it, for
once in your life, admit it.

Al   What are you on about?

Bet   Admit that you're wrong, then I'll tell you.

Al   All right I'm wrong, what is it?

Bet   Read that . . . no, second thoughts, I'll read it.

Al   What is it?

Bet   Ha ha, listen to this.

Al   Read it then.

Bet (*reading from a letter*)   'Dear Guest.' That's me.

Al   Get on with it.

Bet (*reading*)   'Dear Guest, We are delighted to announce
that you are a lucky winner of our Romantic Break
Competition. Take you and your loved one', I suppose
that's you, 'for a night to Romantic Paris.'

Al   Bloody hell.

Bet (*reading*)   'Travel overnight in luxury on North Sea
Ferries, all expenses paid, and stay at the delightful Saint
Germain Hotel. Return journey on North Sea Ferries
rounds off your unforgettable Romantic Break.'

Al   Bloody hell.

Bet   What do you think?

Al   Bloody hell.

Bet   All we have to do is find our spending money.

Al   I knew there'd be a catch.

Bet   Admit that you're wrong about these competitions. 'S not a fix is it?

Al   You won't be able to have time off work, will you?

Bet   Course I will.

Al   Might not have a job when you come back.

Bet   Oh God, give me strength. Don't you think it's great? I've always wanted to go to Paris, haven't you? Don't you think it's great? Are you pleased?

Al   Who are you going to go with?

Bet   You.

Al   I can't go.

Bet   Why?

Al   Well I can't.

Bet   I don't believe you.

Al   I don't want to be trailing around France, do I. Why don't you take Rita?

Bet   All right then, I'll take Rita.

Al   And I hate boats.

Bet   You've never been on one.

Al   There's no way I'd sleep on a boat. I mean what if it's rough? It'd probably sink with my luck. You and Rita go. I'm serious, you and Rita go and have a good time. I'll only ruin it, you know that . . . Besides, I haven't got a passport.

Bet   I haven't.

Al   I've got nothing to wear.

Bet   Well, that's never been a problem before, has it? We'll need to buy a new case, we can't take that one we've got, it looks a mess. I think I'll need a new suit.

Al   We're only going for one day.

Bet   I thought you weren't coming?

Al   I'll go for you.

Bet   No, it's okay, I'll go with Rita. I know you don't like boats. You stay here in your shed, you'll only spoil it. I'll go with Rita, she'll be gobsmacked when I tell her that you want her to go instead of you. Me and Rita in Paris, oooh là là . . . We'll have a dirty weekend, I might come back with a sexy French bloke. I'll nip around and tell her.

Al   Bugger Rita.

Bet   No, it's okay, I understand. You've never been away and you don't want to go. That's okay. Anyway, I don't want to be seen going around Paris with you.

Al   Once you start gallivanting off . . .

Bet   I wonder if Rita's got a passport.

Al   Once you get there you might not want to come back.

Bet   I won't want to come back to you.

Al   You can't speak a word of French.

Bet   I can buy a book.

Al   Probably get mugged.

Bet   I can't wait.

Al   I think you should think about it.

Bet   I have thought about it.

Al   I'm not going.

Bet   Yeah, I know, great. I'm going and you're not, and that's that. I'll go with Rita.

Blackout.

During the blackout **Bet** *exits.* **Al** *moves the chair to the back wall and exits.*

The doorway of the white box becomes a doorway on a ship. The door is hinged and closed, with a porthole.

Music plays: Jacques Brel's 'Vesoul'. The lights come up.

Al *dances on with a large lifebuoy, hangs it from the back wall, and exits.*

Bet *dances on carrying a suitcase. We see her look at the size of the ship in front of her. A light picks her out.*

Bet   Wooow . . . I can't believe it . . . I can't believe I'm doing it . . . I feel like I'm going to burst open with excitement. And the ferry, you should see the size of the ferry! It's massive. I've never seen anything as big in my life. And I can't move for people, people everywhere. A sea of faces and suitcases, cars, buses from all over the place. School parties, tall Dutch kids, a party of pensioners from Newcastle, French students. Everyone is excited to be going back home or abroad like me. I feel free, for the first time in years I feel like I'm game for a laugh, I feel like I can fly. I don't know where *he* is, and I'm not bothered. I've packed everything, passport, travellers' cheques, phrase book, I've packed myself a suit in case I go anywhere. Nice. (*She picks up her case and walks around the stage.*)

The spot goes off.

Al *enters with a suitcase.*

Al   Look out, women and children first.

Bet   Oh you're here, are you?

Al   I've been talking to one of the crew. I went to school with him.

Bet   It's jam-packed full this ferry.

Al   I hope it's not too heavy. It might sink.

Bet   Well you'd better get off, then.

Al   Is this the right boat?

Bet   You should be on that one. Rotterdam.

Al   There's a disco.

Bet   I know.

Al   Two bars.

Bet   Don't go mad, you.

Al   Great int it?

Bet   Giz a cuddle then.

Al   Why, are you cold?

Bet   Yeah.

Al   Put a cardigan on.

Bet   I don't like the look of them lifeboats.

Al   They're all right.

Bet   What number are we?

Al   Five-one sommat . . .

Bet   Right.

Al   I hope I can sleep.

Bet   I don't want the top bunk.

Al   Have you brought the Sealegs?

Bet   You can have the top bunk.

Al   What if I fall off, I'll kill you.

Bet   I've got about ten Sealegs.

Al   Is that enough?

Bet   How many do you want?

Al   It's going to be windy, I think.

Bet   It'll be all right.

Al   Will it?

Bet   These boats sail every night.

Al   Not with us on it.

Bet   It'll be all right. I checked on the telly, it said it was going to be a calm crossing.

Al   I looked and it said moderate.

Bet   Calm it said.

Al   I'm not arguing . . .

Bet   It said calm.

Al   It said moderate.

Bet   Yeah, well, that's what it'll be.

Al   Ar, but what do you call moderate?

Bet   Moderate.

Al   Ar, what's moderate?

Bet   Moderate's like calm, isn't it?

Al   Is it?

Bet   Course it is.

Al   I don't know if I should take any notice of you. You don't know owt.

Bet   Look, try and find the cabin. (*She indicates the suitcase.*) Take this. I'll meet you down on D Deck.

Al   D Deck, where's that?

Bet   Find it.

Al   Ay ay, captain.

He exits, taking the cases with him.

We hear a voice-over.

Voice   Attention, Austroblitz, dinner is now being served in the restaurant on C Deck. Families and coach parties may now dine.

Al *enters.*

Al *and* **Bet** *sit together on chairs upstage right.*

Bet   Massive restaurant, int it?

Al   Not much . . . it's like a bloody hotel.

Bet   That's what it is, a floating hotel.

Al   I don't like sitting with other people.

Bet   Well, what do you want us to do – have dinner in the cabin?

Al   I mean here like this, with these others. We're too close.

Bet   They're a nice couple. They work in Hull at the University.

Al   Where are they going?

Bet   France.

Al   Oh. Like us.

Bet   Yeah.

Al   Have they won it?

Bet   No.

Al   Look at all these people.

Bet   They're going to a little village. Bolougne sommat. They're taking their car to a gîte . . .

Al   Why, what's wrong with it?

Bet   Oh, don't start with your jokes.

Al   We should've kept the car.

Bet   We'll get another one day.

Al   We should've gone away for a few days in England.

Bet   Yeah.

Al   Yeah.

Bet   Where?

Al   Well, we could have had a couple of days at loggerheads.

Bet   You.

Al   What . . .

Bet   You think you're funny.

Al   And I'll tell you sommat you didn't know.

Bet   What?

Al   There's a nudist beach at Filey.

Bet   There isn't?

Al   There is.

Bet   Look shurrup, people can hear you . . .

Al   There is.

Bet   What do you want when they come – soup or fruit juice?

Al   There is.

Bet   People can hear you.

Al   There's a nudist beach at Filey, but you can't see a lot according to form, because they all lie on their fronts. But there's plenty of room to park a bike, apparently.

Bet   I bet they're French.

Al   Where?

Bet   Over there . . .

Al   They're not French are they?

Bet　Well, they're having wine.

Al　Look at that lot there. They're having curry but they're not from India, are they? You do talk some rubbish at times.

Bet　What are you having?

Al　What is there?

Bet　Salad bar.

Al　Oh, I'll have a salad then.

Bet　Or there's curry . . .

Al　I right fancy curry, it looks nice.

Bet　And I think there's chicken pie and chips.

Al　Chicken pie, has it got mushrooms in it?

Bet　How do I know?

Al　I don't know what to have . . . Can you have as much as you want?

Bet　I think so.

Al　Right then. (*He freezes.*)

Bet　I want to die when he goes to the chef three times. Curry, pie and salad and each portion heaped up on his plate, and him smiling like a buffoon. Showing the rest of the ship what he was going to eat.

Al　Bloody lovely that. I'll tell you sommat, there's some silly sods on here only having one meal. I mean we've paid for it, ant we?

Bet　No.

Al　Well, it's there, isn't it? They'll only chuck it to the seagulls if nobody eats it.

Bet　I didn't know where to look.

Al   What's up now, we're supposed to be on holiday, aren't we? I've got some cheese for later, in case we get a bit peckish during the night.

Bet   He had helped himself to half a pound of Edam which he'd wrapped up in a serviette and stuffed in his pocket.

Al   I could get some more if you want it?

Bet   We walk along the plush corridors of the boat, and I detect in the air a faint smell of sick which is a reminder that we are at sea.

Al   It's not bad is it?

Bet   You should've brought a sketch pad, you could have drawn some of this.

Al   Why? You've got a camera, haven't you?

Bet   Do you want to see a film?

Al   No, I had a look earlier. You have to travel backwards. I don't like that.

Bet   Have you never been on a train?

Al   Let's get a drink in . . . (*He turns and freezes.*)

Bet   On D Deck the lounge looks like something from a feature film. I could just imagine voyages in the past. Ships full of barons and countesses all making their way around the world to seek fame and fortune. Everyone dressed for dinner in tuxedo and tie, instead of trainers and T-shirts.

Al   I'm having a pint. What do you want?

Al *brings down the chairs and they sit.*

Bet   We sit in a secluded corner just behind the bar.

Al   Smooth ride, int it. Brilliant. I could get used to this. Hope it stays like this all night. It's as smooth as a baby's arse.

Bet   Don't be sick, will you.

Al   I've had a Sealeg.

Bet   Just take it steady.

Al   I'm only having a pint.

Bet   Right.

Al   What do you want?

Bet   Can I have a white wine?

Al   A bit French, int it?

Bet   Well, what did you expect, we're on holiday, aren't we?

Al   I might have a pint and a chaser, is it all free?

Bet   No.

Al   I'll just have a pint then. (*He moves and freezes.*)

We hear soft piano music: 'Love Story' and 'Moon River'.

Bet   Over by the window the pianist tickles her way through 'Precious Moments' . . . and she chatters and plays requests but no one really listens except me, and I applaud, and I feel really good. Like I was born for this sort of life instead of selling training shoes.

Al   She's killing them songs.

Bet   She's good.

Al   Shall I ask her to play Phil Collins?

Bet   No, leave it. Let's work out what we're going to see, shall we?

Al   Right then. Let's have a plan.

Bet   Let's not have a plan. Let's just see what there is and if we don't see it all we can go back again.

Al   When?

Bet   Another time.

Al   Well, we've got to see the Eiffel Tower, ant we?

Bet   See it, we've got to go up it. We've got tickets.

Al   We haven't got to go up it, have we?

Bet   I thought we'd do all the sights on the first day and then we could just relax on the coming back.

Al   If we do all the sights on the first day we'll need to. How will we go on with eating?

Bet   What do you mean?

Al   I mean, what if there's nowt we like?

Bet   You like bread, don't you?

Al   Yeah. (*He has a small tourist guide to Paris and looks through it.*)

Bet   Well, there's always bread. They make really nice bread.

Al   Arch de Triomphe – we'll want to see that. And the Gare du Nord.

Bet   That's a station.

Al   How do you know?

Bet   Because I've been looking at it every night for the last month.

Al   All right, Marco Polo, keep your shirt on.

Bet   We'll have to bring mi mam sommat back. And I said I'd bring Rita sommat.

Al   We want some duty free and all.

Bet   We'll get some. And we'll have a saunter down the Champs-Elysées.

Al   What is there?

Bet   Shops.

Al   Great.

Bet   Why, what do you want to see?

Al   Well, I wouldn't mind looking at that Pigalle.

Bet   What for?

Al   See what it's like. I heard some bus drivers talking about it down in that shop. They said it was an interesting place to go.

Bet   Oh yeah. I know you.

Al   They said they always take bus trips there. (*Pause.*) Must be interesting, if they always go.

Bet   Well, there's nowt there.

Al   How do you know?

Bet   Well, it's all sex shops and all that, int it?

Al   Is it?

Bet   You know it is.

Al   No, I didn't. I didn't know what it was.

Bet   I mean we don't want to be going all the way to Paris to look at sex shops, do we?

Al   No, suppose not.

Bet   I mean there's lots more to see. Opéra. Louvre.

Al   Oh yeah, opera, great.

Bet   Napoleon's Tomb. Notre Dame.

Al   We can see if that hunchback's in.

Bet   Pompidou Centre, there's loads. We don't want to be spending our time looking at sex shops.

Al   They're sex-mad over there, you know. I should watch 'em. One of the lads had been, at work. He said you couldn't move up there for prostitutes and them transvestites.

Bet   Well, if you want to go, you go, but I'm not.

Al   No, I don't want to go, I was only saying.

Bet   Look, this looks good, Montmartre, Artists' Quarter . . . You'd like that. You might be able to teach 'em a thing or two.

Al   Ha ha . . .

Bet   Oh and by the way, it says everybody tips the waiters and all . . .

Al   I tip.

Bet   Oh yeah.

Al   I do.

Bet   When ever have you tipped anybody?

Al   I can't remember, when I last went out.

Bet   Well, shut up then.

Al   How long is it on the bus when we get there?

Bet   Three hours.

Al   Three hours?

Bet   What's wrong with that?

Al   Nowt.

Pause.

Bet   Typical of you, that, int it?

Al   What?

Bet   Wanting to look at sex shops.

Al   It doesn't bother me.

Bet   Three hours and then we're there. You'll be all right on the bus, it'll suit you.

Al   Why?

Bet   There's a toilet and a video. It's all you need, int it?

Al   Where's the hotel?

Bet   How do I know, I haven't been there before, have I?

Al   I thought you said you'd been studying the map?

Bet   Bloody sex shops? You ought to go learn sommat. They reckon that Frenchmen are the best lovers in Europe.

Al   There's a toilet on the coach is there? That's handy.

Pause.

Bet   She's good on that piano, int she?

Al   She's going through me.

Bet   Oh, you've had a drink, have you?

Al   Yeah, I have, and I'm having another. Do you want one?

Bet   No, I'm all right with one glass of wine.

Al   You're not going to make that last all night, are you?

Bet   Why?

Al   Well, it's embarrassing, int it? Have another.

Bet   It's not. It's what normal people do.

Al   I'm normal.

Bet   Are you?

Al   Don't start it.

Bet   I'm not, I'm just being reasonable.

Al   So can I have another pint or what?

Bet   You don't have to ask me.

Al   I do.

Bet   You don't.

Al   Right. I'm having another pint then.

Bet   Have one then.

Al   I'll be all right, I mean, I'm not going to get legless, am I?

Bet   Aren't you? That'd make a change then.

Al   I'll not have one, then!

Bet   A smooth ride, int it?

Al   No wonder, is there.

Bet   Why?

Al   We're still in Hull. The barman told us. We're waiting for some cargo to arrive from Goole.

Bet   Oh, it must be delayed because of the fog.

Al   Fog, what fog?

Bet   Fog on the M62.

Al   Well, I hope it's not going to follow us. That's all we want, to be lost at sea.

Bet   I hope he shuts them doors properly. I was sat here thinking we were nearly in France.

Al   Well we're not, we're in Hull.

Bet   You don't think it'll be foggy out at sea, do you?

Al   How do I know?

Bet   How can they see in the fog?

Al   The captain's a rabbit.

Bet   You're not funny.

Al   You'll be all right, get some wine down you.

Bet   I don't want a lot. I tell you what, I'll go and play on the fruit machines and then I'll go to the disco, I right fancy a dance.

Al   Well, I'm not dancing with you.

Bet   So what's new?

Al   I'm having another pint.

Bet   That's it, go and get legless, you'll be sick.

Al   Shut up and go and have a dance will you?

A sudden burst of music. Disco lights come up. **Al** *stands upstage. A spotlight picks him out as* **Bet** *dances to the music.*

Down in the disco, I stand like an island watching her parade about. She's enjoying herself, she's having a good time, I'm glad about that. I wish I could join in, I do, I wish I could get up there with her but sommat stops me, I just stand watching 'em all dance, and I'm rooted to the spot, my feet are in concrete, and I'm jealous to death. She's not bothered, she's the oldest one dancin' but she's not bothered, now she's dancin' with some French students, and now she's with a tall Dutch kid – he's only about fifteen, look at her, she's loving it. Look at me, I'm pathetic. I look at a young lass from Antwerp, and I get stupid ideas, I'm thirty-eight, let's be honest, so I tap my foot so as not to look too sad. (*To* **Bet**.) Enjoying it?

Bet   Brilliant.

Al   I'm going to have another, do you want one?

Bet   No, I'm all right, I'm dancing.

Al   Bloody hell.

Bet   Int it brilliant?

Al   An hour later she's still dancin' and the boat rocks, and dips and we are out there, out into the North Sea, out into all that blackness.

Bet   I feel a bit queasy.

Al   What?

Bet   I feel a bit queasy.

Al   There's no wonder, is there? I thought you were having a stroke.

Bet   What?

Al   It was a joke, the way you were dancing.

Bet   I fancy a bit of fresh air.

Al   Have you seen the time?

Bet   Come on, let's go on deck.

Al   It's windy out there.

Bet   Oh come on, you fart, let's live a bit.

Al   I thought you felt queasy.

Bet   Let's get some fresh air, I'm boiling.

The lights change. The disco music fades. Wind is heard as the lights go to blue out on deck. A cloud effect gives a sense of movement.

Bet *exits and immediately returns with two windjammers.*

Al *brings the chairs centre stage. Both* **Al** *and* **Bet** *reach for the windjammers which they try and put on against the wind.* **Al** *reaches up and sets the hanging light swinging to give the impression of the boat's movement. The wind fades.*

Put your coat on . . .

Al   It's only plastic.

Bet   Windy.

Al   Windy . . . is that an understatement?

Bet   This'll blow the cobwebs off us.

Al   It'll blow us off if we don't watch it.

Bet   It's a bit scary, int it?

Al   Do you feel any better?

Bet   A bit . . . it was too stuffy. I haven't danced like that in years.

Al   Nobody has.

Bet   I want fresh air.

Al   Well, it doesn't come any fresher than this.

Bet   It's great . . .

Al   Look at the waves.

Bet   This doesn't look calm to me . . .

Al   No, it dun't look calm to me either. In fact I'd say it looks bloody rough . . . look out for the icebergs.

Bet   Moderate to rough?

Al   I suppose so.

Bet   Bloody hell. I hope it doesn't get much rougher.

Al   Well, I think it will.

Bet   How do you know?

Al   There's a forecast on the wall near that Information Desk. A weather chart thing.

Bet   Oh yeah . . .

Al   It said that erratic winds were expected to come down from Poland, and cause havoc in the North Sea. That's why I've had all that to drink – if it gets bad I'm gonna sleep through it.

Bet   Why didn't you tell me?

Al   Why, you don't feel sick do you?

Bet   Shall we go back?

Al   What for? We're all right just yet. Just take deep breaths if you feel bad.

Bet   Let's go back.

Al   You're all right. Nothing to be frightened of. Whooo, I'll tell you what, all this fresh air's making me a bit woozy. Whooo, brilliant. God, look at the clouds.

Bet   Where?

Al   Where? There in the bloody sky. Look at the clouds. Frightening.

Bet   It's going to be stormy.

Pause.

Al   Look at the clouds.

Pause.

Bet   Don't go too near the edge, will you? Be dead easy for somebody to fall off, wouldn't it?

Al   Yeah.

Bet   Just don't go near the edge.

Al   How do you feel?

Bet   Sick.

Al   Take deep breaths from your mouth.

Bet   Thanks. (*She breathes deeply.*)

Al   Better?

Bet   No.

Al   Just keep breathing.

Bet   Yeah.

Al   Do you want me to hold you?

Bet   No, I want you to leave me alone. Oh dear . . . have I gone pale?

Al Pale green, yeah.

Bet Oh dear . . .

Al Just keep breathing.

Bet Don't you feel bad?

Al I do a bit.

Bet You shouldn't've had all that food. I knew you'd be sick.

Al Give it a rest for a minute, will you?

Bet You were like a bloody animal, I didn't know where to look.

Al Ohhh, I feel bad.

Bet I've got no sympathy.

Al I need a pee.

Bet Let's go back then.

Al No . . . I'll have to have one out.

Bet Don't be pathetic . . .

Al Nobody'll know.

Bet I will.

Al I'll have one over the side.

Bet You won't.

Al It must be all the water.

Bet Oh yeah, it'll not be the beer, will it? You always have to overdo it.

Al Now we know what moderate is.

Bet I feel a bit bad again.

Al Did you have a Sealeg?

Bet There was one left.

Al   You should've had a brandy. That's supposed to calm your stomach.

Bet   Oh . . .

Al   Are you all right?

Bet   No, I feel awful.

Al   Do you feel sick?

Bet   Yeah.

Al   I feel all right now.

Bet   I'm going to be sick.

Al   Keep swallowing.

Bet . I am.

Al   What do you want me to do?

Bet   Oh hell . . . I think I'm gonna . . .

Al   Are you all right?

Bet *makes her way to the side of the boat upstage and heaves off-stage.*

Bet   Uuurrrrrghgh . . .

Al   Are you all right?

Bet   Uuurghhhhhh . . .

Al   Oh dear.

Bet   Urghhhhhhhh . . .

Al   Speak up when you're through.

Bet   Uuuurghhhhh . . .

Al   Get it up, it'll be better once it's up.

Bet   Oh, I hate being sick.

Al   I do.

Bet   Urgghghghhhh . . .

Al You're making me feel bad.

Bet Don't help me, will you?

Al What do you want me to do?

Bet (*recovering from sea sickness*) Oh . . .

Al All right.

Bet I felt fine then it just came.

Al I don't know, I can't take you anywhere, can I?

Bet Oh . . . typical.

Al What?

Bet Nothing ever happens to you, does it?

Al You're joking, aren't you?

Bet Oh, I feel better.

Al What have you been eating?

Bet It must be them chocolates. I tret myself to some chocolates before we got on. For a little treat.

Al You and them treats. You didn't offer me one.

Bet It was my treat.

Al Serves you right then.

Bet God's judgement on me.

Al You feel okay, can I get you owt?

Bet No.

Al Better?

Bet (*recovering*) That's a lot better.

Al It sounded like it . . .

Bet One good thing, I've still got my own teeth . . .

Al   It's a good job, int it, otherwise they'd be in Holland by now.

Bet   Is it calming down?

Al   Feel better?

Bet   Yeah. This is with you.

Al   What?

Bet   Wanting to come out here in this weather . . .

Al   You wanted some fresh air, I was happy enough watching the disco.

Bet   Let's go back. I want to read for a bit. (*She moans.*)

Al   Oh . . . go then . . . I'm going to stay out here.

Bet   I can't leave you out here, can I?

Al   Why, what am I gonna do, jump off?

Bet   Oh, don't start . . .

Al   I know you'll never understand, but I feel ashamed.

Bet   Ashamed? What, of behaving like a pig? You do it all the time.

Al   Of this holiday. Everybody on here's paid and we're here for free.

Bet   So what?

Al   I haven't taken you on holiday for two years and the only holiday we have is one that we've won.

Bet   It doesn't matter.

Al   Course it matters.

Bet   There's nothing wrong with winning.

Al   I've always wanted to take you somewhere nice, and we go and win a bloody holiday. I mean, where have we been before? Grange-over-Sands in a holiday flat and you hated it.

Bet It doesn't matter.

Al What's going to happen next year?

Bet Next year'll be different.

Al Will it? What are you gonna win next year?

Bet What's wrong with you? Just enjoy it.

Al Or the year after that . . . because you know we can't afford to go away. And that's why you do them competitions – to get back at me.

Bet I don't.

Al You do.

Bet Let's take a day at a time.

Al I've got nowt to look forward to, have I?

Bet Give it a miss, will you?

Al Bloody nowt.

Bet Stop feeling sorry for yourself and grow up.

Al Do you want to know sommat?

Bet Go on . . .

Al I'm fed up . . .

Bet Well, throw yourself overboard then, and end it all.

Al Do you think I haven't thought about it?

Bet Do it then. You're too scared to do it.

Al I will do it and then you'd be in a mess.

Bet Would I?

Al You would.

Bet I wouldn't.

Al   What a bloody country we live in. We've had'a win a bloody holiday.

Bet   So do thousands of others. It's not just me and you. Can we forget this and go inside? I'm frozen.

Al   You go, I'm stopping here. (*Pause.*) Go then, go and read a book. (*Pause; shouting.*) It's my holiday – I want to do what I want.

Bet   Oh, I could just push you off this boat and think I'd done nowt . . . Push you off and start my life again. You'd be down there floating about with a belly full of beer.

Al (*seeing a light at sea*)   England.

Bet   What?

Al   England there, look at it. Just an island int it? I don't think it'll ever get sorted out now.

Bet   It's not our worry, is it?

Al   No . . . Have you looked at the people lately? Have you looked at the people in the streets? Don't you think they look sad?

Bet   Not as sad as you.

Al   I think they look sad.

Bet   I wish you'd never come.

Al   I know.

Bet   I wish I'd come with Rita.

Al   I told you to. But you never listen to me.

Bet   You spoil everything.

Al   I've never done anything right for you, have I? Not in ten years.

Bet   Let's go back inside, we can't talk about this here.

Pause.

Al   Come here . . .

Bet   No . . .

Al   Come here, you . . .

Bet   No . . .

Al   Come here, it's a holiday.

Bet *goes to* **Al** *and they hug. He looks at her.*

Al   Sorry.

Bet   What for?

Pause. In the silence they place the chairs back to back centre stage and sit sideways on them so that they are facing the audience.

Al   For going on . . .

Bet   It's okay.

Al   Do you want to know sommat?

Bet   What?

Al   Your breath stinks of sick . . .

A beat.

Bet   Thanks.

Pause. **Al** *attempts to put his arm around* **Bet**. *Finally she succumbs.*

Al (*excited*)   Paris . . . bloody hell.

French music plays: 'Les Bourgeois' by Jacques Brel and Jean Corti. As the music plays the lights fade, and just before the lights reach blackout **Al** *waves goodbye to England.*

Blackout.

Act Two

A large Renoir painting fills the entire stage. Two Parisian chairs are placed upstage right. They are the only props used in Paris, and can fold away. The hanging light is no longer visible.

Can-can music plays as **Bet** *and* **Al** *enter and sit on the chairs. They are tired from looking around. They do not take in the audience yet. The music stops.*

Al   I'm tired out. I mean, we've walked all over.

Bet   Well, I told you we should have got the Métro.

Al   I'm not getting no Métro.

Bet   Why?

Al   People get mugged on the Métro.

Bet   They don't.

Al   People get mugged.

Bet   They don't.

Al   They do.

Bet   Millions of people use it every day . . .

Al   Ar, and some of 'em get mugged.

Bet   Bloody hell, you . . .

Al   It's bigger than I thought it would be . . .

Bet   Ar, it's bigger than your shed, int it?

Al   Just about . . .

Bet   What do you think to the hotel?

Al   Not bad, and two toilets, that's handy . . .

Bet   It's a bidet . . .

Al   I know . . .

Bet   And that champagne in our room was great, wasn't it? I'll take that home. (*She takes in the audience.*) We're up by the Trocadéro, from here you can see the Eiffel Tower.

Al   You can see the Eiffel Tower from anywhere.

Bet   And the Seine.

Al   Can't move for kids. Are we going to have a bite? (*He brings the chairs downstage right.*)

Bet   He doesn't want to sit outside the café, so despite the soaring heat we go and sit inside the Café Trocadéro . . . We gaze up at the large menu on the wall . . .

Al   And we settle near a posh French bloke who's eating an omelette.

Bet   Do you want an omelette?

They sit on two chairs, giving the impression that the restaurant is full. They are pleased at being in the restaurant.

Al   The menu is all in French.

Bet   What did you expect?

Al   Well, I thought . . .

Bet   Nice, int it?

Al   It's all rate, yeah.

Bet   Ohhh, my feet. I'm ready for this. Ohhh.

Al   You choose sommat for me, I can't follow it.

Bet   Let's having sommat daring, shall we? Can you see what there is?

Al   I can hardly see the wall.

Bet   You need some new glasses, I've told you.

Al   If you can't tell what it says we can have a Big Mac.

Bet   I read the menu and make out something about fish and steak. I think. It'll be a laugh, we'll have steak and fish. Int it nice?

Al   What about an omelette?

Bet   It doesn't say omelette.

Al   He's got an omelette.

Bet   Take your pick, fish or steak.

Al   Is that all there is?

Bet   You can have soup.

Al   I'll have steak. Well done, you never know what you're eating. Where's the loo?

Bet   How do I know?

Al (*whispering*)   I'll try and find the loo. Hey, look at that – they've got a different menu to us. They've got a different menu to us! Crafty sods, I bet you can have omelette on that menu.

Bet   Have steak now.

Al   Crafty sods, one menu for them and one for the tourists. That'd never happen in England.

Bet   Go to the toilet.

Al   I right fancy an omelette. Shall I say sommat?

Bet   You're having steak. Make do with that.

Al   Crafty sods. (*To the waiter.*) Hey, I say, mate . . . (*He whistles.*)

Bet   Go to the toilet and leave it.

Al   Crafty sods.

Bet   I thought you were going to try and be romantic?

Al   I am trying.

Al *walks upstage looking for the toilet, which he finds is simply a hole in the ground. During the following,* **Bet** *and* **Al** *address the audience separately.*

Bet So he's in the loo, and I try through smiles and points to order. (*To an imaginary waiter.*) Bonjour. Une Steak Tartare. Une poisson and sauce. With two cups of tea. Tea . . . please tea . . . merci. And all the while I'm struggling with my little book and bad grammar, I know and he knows that the waiter speaks better English than uz. 'Merci,' he snaps, a bit over-friendly like, and floats away to a table where he is relieved to serve someone French. And I hope I've ordered the right thing, and I sit and watch and dread his return from la toilette.

Al In le toilet I'm confused. I've wandered down two flights of stairs to get here and when I've arrived all I see is a hole in the ground, and two foot pads.

Bet Around the café I catch polite glances and smiles and whispers which I translate into 'She's English', followed by a little laugh. And every Chanel suit and elegant two-piece is looking at me.

Al And I still stand, looking, looking at this hole in the earth.

Bet The men draw on their Gauloises, and the women sip their Muscadet and chat and laugh and smoke, and I can't believe that I'm in Paris, this is the colour and excitement of a wonderful city. And I dread his return. More women enter the café, slim, elegant women, expensive women and the intoxication draws me into an insecurity. They look at me and know something is wrong. They seem to know I don't belong, and I think I hear them say that my suit is from British Home Stores.

Al I stand still, silent, thinking, pondering. I wait for a while, I go through the motions in my head. I make it appear as if I've been, I time myself in my head. But there is no way. The hole in the ground still beckons, but I can't oblige.

Bet   And suddenly I'm desperate for him to return, he's been there too long, he always takes too long. Too many eyes now, too many slanting smiles, lip corners twist, and necks crane to look at me, and why doesn't he come back? What can he be doing in there? And then the meal arrives. Mine a beautiful piece of fish cooked in white wine with a sauce to match, too nice to eat really, his a plate of raw mince meat with a raw egg in the middle.

Al   I make my way back up the spiral staircase, stunned and slightly worried.

Al *returns to the table.*

Bet   Where've you been?

Al   Wait till you have to go. (*He looks at the steak.*) I look at the plate of raw meat.

Bet   Get it.

Al   What is it?

Bet   Just don't make a fuss, I didn't know, just eat it, everybody's looking.

Al   There's no wonder, is there? I've got some horse's giblets on my plate.

Bet   Just get it.

Al   I can't eat this, I wouldn't give it to a pig.

Bet   I thought you were hungry.

Al   What are you trying to do, kill me?

Bet   Just eat it. I'm sorry, all right I didn't know what it was.

Al   I don't know what it is.

Bet   For goodness sake, eat it, we can't send it back, can we?

Al   And so I eat it. Cold raw mince meat. I eat it. I mix the egg into the mince and eat it. Slowly I can feel the meat fighting its way to my stomach. The egg eases its way down, a little hiccup (*He hiccups.*), a moment of panic, a worry, a serviette wipes a bubble from my lips. But all is secure. A sip of tea and it's all gone. I eat it all. I'm so hungry I could eat it again. And the man with the omelette looks enviously at my empty plate. I wipe my mouth and sip my English tea. (*He belches loudly.*) Ah . . . nice . . .

Bet   Don't.

Al   That's what they do over here.

Bet (*standing up to leave*)   With some relief we depart.

Al   Bon voyage. (*He takes the chairs upstage right.*)

Bet   And after l'addition, he leaves a tip.

Al   Hey, keep away from mucky women.

Bet   And out on to the streets. The noisy, busy streets.

Al   We stand on the Place de Trocadéro and take in the sights.

Bet   We've nearly done 'em all . . .

Al   Great.

Bet   In just under six hours.

Al   It must be a record. (*A pause while he looks out at the sights.*) Place de la Concorde over there, Invalides, been there. Up there, Arc de Triomphe.

Bet   Do you like it?

Al   Well, it's different, int it?

Bet   But do you like it?

Al   Yeah, course I do.

Bet   Let's go up the Eiffel Tower.

Al   What for?

Bet   See Paris.

Al   We can see it from here.

Bet   Oh come on, come on, please . . . We've got tickets.

Al   Do you want to?

Bet   Yeah, come on. Everybody goes up the Tower.

Al   So we queue for thirty minutes in front of a school party from Plymouth who talk non-stop about some French girls they have met, and Madonna, and I pretend to be foreign, and these kids giggle and push, and the only thing I hope is that they are not in our lift because if they are I'll swing for 'em. There's only one thing I hate more than kids . . . and it's heights.

Bet   We agree, as is the compromise of my life, that we won't go right to the top. And on the first station I buy my mother a flag with the Tower on.

Al   Where's she gunna put that?

Bet   He buys a model of the Tower in a snow storm.

Al   It's cheap but I like it.

Bet   And there we are, overlooking a jigsaw of beauty.

They stand centre stage. **Bet** *looks out towards the audience.*

Bet   What a view – hey, get that painted.

Al   Look at that . . . All the streets are in straight lines.

Bet   That's to stop another revolution, int it? You could get a tank down them streets.

Al   Bloody hell.

Bet   I'm not thick.

Al   I know that. (*He moves away.*)

Bet Great tower, int it?

Al (*looking elsewhere*) Three hundred metres high.

Bet Really?

Al It was built as part of the World's Fair. To celebrate the centenary of the Revolution.

Bet Hey . . .

Al What?

Bet Look at us in Paris.

Al They were going to demolish it in nineteen-o-nine.

Bet That's not true, is it?

Al Course it is.

Bet How come you know all this?

Al It says so here on this plaque. (*Reading.*) 'It is a unique masterpiece of equilibrium and lightness despite weighing seven thousand tons.'

Bet Look at you.

Al What?

Bet You're enjoying it, aren't you?

Al Why do you put up with me?

Bet Answer me. Are you enjoying it?

Al Yeah.

Bet Well, why don't you tell me?

Al I do.

Bet You don't, you think you do, you think you talk to me and tell me things but you don't. You keep it inside.

Al Where shall we go next?

Bet I thought you'd seen enough.

Al Come on, tourist guide, take us somewhere.

Bet Give us a kiss then, in Paris.

Al What for?

Bet Because the tourist guide needs one.

Al No.

Bet I'll throw you off the Tower if you don't.

Al *politely pecks her on the cheek.*

Well, thanks a lot.

Al `You're welcome.

Bet Your breath smells awful.

Al I'm not surprised, it's them horse giblets.

Bet I don't know how women can resist you.

The lights change to indicate the Louvre. The Mona Lisa is simply a power white light pointing downward.

Al After the Tower we nip across to the Louvre. (*He sees something.*) Woow, look at that.

Bet What?

Al Woow . . .

Bet Calm down . . . everybody's looking . . .

Al Bloody hell.

Bet Haven't you seen it before?

Al Not in real life . . . (*To the audience.*) Mona Lisa.

Bet Small, int it?

Al Look at it.

Bet I thought it would be bigger.

Al (*breathlessly*) It's fantastic.

Bet Small, int it?

Al Ohhh God, it's brilliant.

Bet I didn't think you'd like it, I thought you'd say it was rubbish.

Al But just look at it, look at the colour. I've never seen owt like it.

Bet It's no better than the others to me.

Al Oh, you're joking. It's a masterpiece.

Bet What makes it better then?

Al Look at the colours. See them others, same period. But they're very crude compared to this. You see that smile, wherever you stand it looks like she's smiling at you.

Bet She is smiling at me . . .

Al She was a whore, wan't she?

Bet Was she?

Al At first they thought she was an official's wife.

Bet You're good, aren't you?

Al But they reckon she was a bit of a goer.

Bet That's why she's smiling?

Al He's tried to blend all the colours, you see, like smoke. Bloody hell, it's brilliant.

Bet You couldn't do that, then?

Al Not in a million years.

Bet Keep trying.

Al I will do.

Bet (*turning, pointing to another painting*) I like that one, and that one. Oh, and I like that one.

They look at the art.

Al   Renoir, and Manet.

Bet   And that one, and that one.

Al   Cézanne, and Monet.

Bet   Ooh, I like that one, and that one . . .

Al   Matisse, and Magritte.

Bet   We walked for miles through the Louvre.

Al   I like that one and that one.

Bet (*stopping*)   I don't like that one.

Al   And that one and that one.

Bet   I don't like all that modern stuff, anybody could do it.

Al   What, even me?

Bet   You do do it, don't you?

Al   I think we should go.

Bet   Why?

Al   Because we're never going to see it all, are we? So we might as well stop looking now.

Bet   We've seen a lot, though.

Al   We might as well stop looking now.

Bet   All right, don't be so nasty.

Al   The more we see, the more we don't know.

Bet   Well, you know what you like 'n' that's all that matters.

Al   Come on, let's get out.

Bet   We can have another ten minutes, if you want . . .

Al   Ten minutes? You need ten years. Let's go.

Bet   All right, keep your shirt on. We'll have another coffee.

Al Who's paying? We're going through the money, you know.

Bet I'll pay.

Al Is it my treat?

Bet Yeah.

Al Brilliant . . . across from the Louvre, stop at a café and rest from an overdose of art. I mean, I'm just speechless.

Bet (*bringing him a chair*) The Parisians are a bit funny though, right offhand.

Al Well, it's their city, int it? They don't want louts like us messing it up.

Bet My feet are killing me. I'm gonna have to get a plaster . . . And I want to take Rita's lad a T-shirt, there's some over there with Paris written on.

Al Well, what shall I do?

Bet Well, you sit here and wait.

Al Eh?

Bet You wait here and order me a cup of tea. And I fancy a bun, or sommat.

Al Eh?

Bet Yeah.

Al A bun.

Bet Or a cream cake. I could just eat a cream cake.

Al What, you mean stay here on me own, by myself?

Bet Yeah.

Al Oh, right.

Bet You'll be all right.

Al You'd better give me the book then.

Bet What for? You'll be all right – besides, I'm going to need the book, aren't I?

Al You're only going to get a T-shirt.

Bet I don't know what 'plaster' is though, do I?

Al Well, what am I supposed to do?

Bet You'll be all right. Just say 'tea'. They'll know what you mean.

Al Oh, right.

Bet *goes upstage.* **Al** *sits alone. He is extremely uncomfortable.*

So I sit, like a lemon on my own and wait outside the Café Rousseau.

Bet I'm looking at some T-shirts near the Louvre.

Al I hope she int going to be long.

Bet It's a change to be by myself, just looking, just wandering.

Al A waiter appears. (*He waves.*) Eghhermp . . . I'll let him go, get the next one.

Bet It's nice to be French for five minutes.

Al I play with an ashtray. Try and find it interesting.

Bet I try a bit of French – bonjour, je regardez. Eh, it works.

Al Beautiful café, int it? Across from here, I can see a water fountain, and through the water I just about make out the words Comédie Française. It certainly will be. I ignore everyone's nods and glances, I pretend I'm not here, another waiter, I blank him, another, I cough, another, a waitress, she's nice. She's coming straight for me, oh no . . . oh no . . . I reach for a newspaper, pretend to read . . . it's French. I can't read that . . . I'll leave it . . . She's coming over, slowly coming over, her hair cascading in the sunlight, slow motion, she comes to my table. I wish I was dead . . .

I'm sat here smiling like a moron. Oh no . . . Oh . . . 'Bonjour,' she says . . . bonjour, what sort of bloody word is that, 'Bonjour'?

Bet   Bonjour!

Al   'Bonjour,' she says.

Bet   Bonjour!

Al   Bonjour?

Bet   Oh, it's great, int it?

Al   She may as well talk to a stone . . .

Bet   Bonjour!

Al   And I run for it.

Bet   Merci, au revoir.

Al   I make a dash while the waitress bonjours someone else, 'Bonjour', she says to an older woman who passes with one of them poodles. And I'm up and away out of the danger zone . . . (*He takes the chair upstage left and walks quickly around the stage to* **Bet**.) Oohhhhh, hang on.

Bet   What are you doing?

Al   Café was shut.

Bet   It wasn't.

Al   It was just closing, half-day apparently.

Bet   Can't you do anything.

Al   Nobody came, I'd been sat there an hour.

Bet   Twenty minutes.

Al   Nobody came.

Bet   I can't leave you to do anything, can I?

Al   Be fair, I'm playing away from home here.

Bet   Yeah, I think I'll put you on the transfer list.

Al   I waved but they all ignored me. You know what they say about the French. I mean, they've got all this art and half of 'em are pig ignorant.

Bet   And you're not.

Al   I'd got it all worked out in my head. Je suis un croissant avec thé.

Bet   I am a croissant with tea? Bloody hell. It's a good job you came away, they might have thought you were an escaped lunatic.

Al   Well, I can only just talk English, can't I . . . I'm all right with French.

Bet   To look . . . je regardez. L'addition . . . the bill. Je voudrais café noir . . . I would like a black coffee.

Al   You're brilliant.

Bet   You just have to try.

Al   Have you just learnt that?

Bet   Yeah.

Al   You're brilliant, aren't you?

Bet   Come on, let's go back to the hotel.

Al   Where is it from here?

Bet   Up this way . . .

Al   It's miles.

Bet   We can get the Métro . . .

Al   I'm not getting the Métro.

Bet   Why not?

Al   I'm not getting the Métro, you get it if you want, I'm not arguing about it, but I'm not getting the Métro, no way. I don't like it.

Bet   You've never been on it.

Al   I don't like small spaces, I panic.

Bet   Your shed's a small space.

Al   It's not underground, is it?

Bet   Hey, well, put your hand up if you want another cup of coffee.

Al (*putting his hand up*)   Ool alla la . . .

Bet   Bon.

Al   Très bon.

Bet   Oui.

Al   Oui, oui.

Bet   Merci.

Al   Bonjour.

Bet   Bon voyage.

Al   D'accord.

Bet   Bloody hell . . .

They move to the chairs, **Bet** *upstage right,* **Al** *upstage left.*

Al   Back at the hotel we change for our night in Paris . . . massive room, int it? There's this massive bed, nearly as big as our house . . .

Bet   Don't exaggerate.

Al   I'm not . . .

Bet   Have you had a bath?

Al   Course I have . . . and I've washed it after I've finished.

Bet   There's a maid.

Al   Is there?

Bet   She'll come and pull the bed covers back. That fruit looked nice, didn't it?

Al I had an apple.

Bet And did you see them chocolates?

Al No.

Bet Yes, this morning there were two chocolates on the bed. I ate mine . . .

Al I didn't have mine . . .

Bet No, I had yours.

Al I don't know about you, but I'm tired out . . . I could just go to bed.

Bet Ooo là là . . .

Al Hey, you stop that . . . It's like 'It's a Knock Out', all this chasing about.

Bet Are you ready? Let's get out there . . .

Al I'll need a bloody holiday when we get back . . .

Bet Right. Come on, let's hit the town.

Al Right. Pigalle, here we come . . .

The lights change to indicate Pigalle.

Bet We're only going to look . . .

Al Well, everybody does, don't they? Let's be honest . . .

Bet We take a taxi . . .

Al A taxi?

Bet As a treat, and we arrive at a Moulin Rouge thriving with bus trips, all of them wandering around Pigalle.

They use the audience as the sex supermarket.

Al Seedy, int it?

Bet We pass a sex supermarket three times but we don't go in . . .

Al We're not like that, are we? . . . You can't move for tourists up in Pigalle, and they're English, most of 'em.

Bet Don't you go out of my sight, I don't like it up here.

Al You'll be all rate wi' me.

Bet Oh ar . . .

Al Nobody'll bother you while you're wi' me or they'll get a fat lip.

Bet It's weird up here . . . sex shops all over . . . weird . . .

Al It's rate . . .

Bet It's weird . . . Eh, look at them pictures . . .

Al It's rate, just keep hold of your handbag . . .

Bet Do you want to hold it for me?

Al Not up here I don't.

Bet We couldn't afford the Folles.

Al Bloody rip off, sixty quid meal and show . . .

Music plays quietly: 'I Am What I Am' from La Cage aux Folles.

They bring the chairs centre stage and sit. A spotlight picks them out.

Bet So we picked a club out of the blue and we've booked for an evening at Madame Arthur's, we don't know what it'll be like, but it's nice, clean inside, but it's dark and hot, like being in an oven, and it's sleazy but we like it, an' the waiters speak English. They bring us some wine . . .

Al Well, here's to Paris . . . cheers.

Bet Cheers.

Al And we sit and drink cheap red plonk.

Bet And he kisses me.

Al And food arrives and more wine.

Bet And I kiss him.

Al   And we have oysters, prawns and snails.

Bet   I left mine.

Al   And then the lights went down. We didn't know what to expect, did we?

Bet   And an hour later . . .

Al   The whole club is throbbing, clapping, I'm telling you I never thought I'd sit and watch grown blokes dressed up as women for three hours. It was brilliant, and we're laughing, aren't we? Laughing.

Bet   I'm crying with laughing.

Al   Everybody is . . .

Bet   And what's funny is their legs, they shave their legs.

Al   She can't stop laughing at their legs, and they're in these awful tights, and the scenery shakes, and the music, the bloody music is awful, you can see the speakers shaking.

Bet   And two wigs don't fit.

Al   And one's got the wrong wig on . . .

Bet   But they keep coming out. Oh dear, funny.

Al   And you love 'em.

Bet   They charm you.

Al   You love 'em. I never thought I'd sit through owt like that, but I'll tell you this, they worked bloody hard.

Pause. The music stops. Silence.

Bet   Wasn't it weird?

Al   You look nice.

Bet   What?

Al   I said you look nice.

Bet   Who?

Al   You.

Bet   I don't, my hair's all gone a mess.

Al   You do . . .

Bet   You're drunk.

Al   So what?

Bet   So am I! How many bottles have we had?

Al   I think I'll try and get another.

Bet   Don't bother.

Pause.

You look really nice, Al.

Al   What?

Bet   You look nice, attractive . . .

Al   No, no.

Bet   What?

Al   Say it again.

Bet   What?

Al   That other bit.

Bet   What?

Al   Say it again.

Bet (*giggling*)   It again.

Al   No.

Bet   No.

Al   No, just say what you said.

Bet   I said I think you look nice, Al.

Al   You never call me my name.

Bet   I do.

Al   You don't, you don't, you never call me my name.

Bet   Don't I?

Al   You never call me my name.

Bet   I think I do.

Al   I never call you your name.

Bet   What is my name?

Al   Dunno, I've forgot.

Bet   You spoil everything, that could have been really nice and you spoil everything.

Al   I don't, Bet . . . I don't. See, I do know your name.

Bet   You'll have forgotten it by the time you sober up, though.

They begin to move away from their seats. **Al** *takes chairs right.*

Al   That evening we stagger out of Madame Arthur's at half-past one in the morning . . . and we're exhausted, aren't we? Absolutely tired out . . . It'd be easier to go to the moon and back . . .

Bet   We're not going to walk, are we?

Al   Are we hell, we'll get the Métro. Un carnet si'l vous plaît.

Bet   Bloody hell. How did you know that?

Al   I've been working it out all day.

Bet   So we get on the Métro back to St Germain.

They stand centre stage with their arms in the air, holding the imaginary handles. **Bet** *holds on to* **Al**. *The lights change and they rock to simulate moving on the train.*

Al   Not bad is it?

Bet   I'm not too keen this late at night. I don't like to be hemmed in.

Al   Have you ever been on the Underground in London?

Bet   I've never been to London.

Al   What?

Bet   No.

Al   Don't look now but I think we're being watched.

Bet   Where? (*She looks around.*)

Al   I said don't look.

Bet   They might be pickpockets.

Al   Might be.

Bet   Do you think they know we're English?

Al   I think they probably do, yeah.

Bet   I've just seen 'em take that bloke's wallet.

Al   Don't panic.

Bet   What shall we do? They might have guns.

Al   Don't panic.

Bet   Do sommat, Al.

Al   Hang on. They aren't bothering us, are they?

Bet   They're still looking at us, though.

Al   Just ignore 'em.

Bet   They're looking at us. Look away from 'em.

Al   You look away from 'em then.

Bet   I am.

Al   I said we should never have come on the Métro.

Bet   They're coming over here.

Al   Oh bloody hell.

Bet   Look at 'em, they're like gypsies.

Al   Don't look at 'em.

Bet   They're coming, Al.

Al   Just move this way.

Bet   I can't move.

Al   Watch your handbag.

Bet   Where's the passports?

Al   You've got mine.

Bet   Do sommat.

Al   What?

Bet   Sommat.

Al   Oh hell. You and them competitions. I could kill you.

Bet   Do sommat.

Al *suddenly breaks away from* **Bet** *and turns to the would-be muggers.*

Al (*screaming*)   Arrrgh . . . right, that's it. Come on then, come and get it if you want some of this you French bastards . . . come on . . . I'm English and I'm not having it. Come on all of you, I'll take you all on . . . come on . . . What are you looking at, come on, come on . . . You stinking sods, I'll knock your bloody teeth out.

Bet   Everyone on the Métro is looking at him.

Al   Come on, you've picked the wrong 'un here . . .

Bet   The muggers get off the Métro and run up the platform.

Al   Come on . . .

Bet   The whole of our carriage get off.

Al   Look at 'em . . .

Bet   We are the only two people left on the Métro.

Al   That did it.

Bet   Scared half of Paris to bloody death. Are you okay?

Al   I'm shaking like a leaf. Oh, my legs have gone, look at me shaking.

Bet   I wonder if they were muggers.

Al   Dun't matter, does it? If they were they've been chased off.

Bet   And if they weren't?

Al   Well, if they weren't there's four French blokes who think there's an English nutcase on the Métro . . . Oh, I'm sweating with fear . . .

Bet   What would you have done, Al, if they'd've come for you?

Al   Messed my pants, probably . . .

The lights change to indicate Nôtre Dame. Solemn organ music plays. It is the next morning and they have to prepare to leave Paris.

Al *exits and brings on their suitcases.*

Bet *looks around.* **Al** *finds* **Bet** *lost in thought in Nôtre Dame.*

Al   What are you playing at in here . . . we're gunna miss the bus . . .

Bet   We can't go home without coming to Nôtre Dame, can we? Kneel down.

Al   No, I'm not into that!

Bet   Kneel down.

Al   No.

Bet   Come on.

Al   I'd never do this at home.

Bet   We're not at home.

Al Ohh.

Pause.

Bet Just say a prayer.

Al I don't believe in owt.

Bet You can just say a prayer, can't you?

Al Yeah, I can do, I suppose.

Silence as they pray. **Al** *attempts to attract* **Bet**'s *attention.*

(*Finally.*) What are you praying about?

Bet I'm not telling you.

Al Why not?

Bet Just say one. (*Pause.*) Amen . . . (*Pause.*) Come on . . . come on . . . How long are you going to be?

Al I haven't finished yet. (*Pause.*) Amen.

Bet You always have to overdo it, don't you?

Al I don't.

Bet What did you pray for?

Al That we didn't miss the boat.

Bet I just prayed for sommat nice . . .

Al Who do you think was listening, Father Christmas?

Bet Don't make fun. What did you pray for?

Al I just wondered what it was all about, why we want to have everything. I just wondered why, if this is all there is, why aren't we nice to each other?

Bet Bloody hell.

Al It's just made me think, that's all.

Bet I thought that you didn't believe.

Al Well . . .

Bet   Well what?

Al   Well, there's got to be sommat, ant there?

Bet   I suppose so.

Al   There's got to be sommat. I mean, we can't just be here alone, can we?

Bet   You never know.

Al   It'd be a bit frightening if we were just here on uz own. There's got to be sommat, hasn't there? Otherwise it is a sorry mess.

Bet   Makes you think, doesn't it? There's so many good things in the world and I bet hardly anybody really sees 'em, we're lucky to be here, aren't we?

Al   Very lucky, thanks to Bella.

Pause. They move right and sit.

Do you wanna know what I've been thinking lately?

Bet   No.

Al   Shall I tell you?

Bet   I don't know if I can take it.

Al   Just lately I've been wondering what my life'll be like when you've gone.

Bet   What do you mean, 'gone'? What do you mean, when I'm gone?

Al   You know, gone, died. Passed on. I looked at that tomb and I imagined I saw your name on it and I thought, God, my life'll be a mess whenever Bet's not here.

Bet   Oh, you're morbid.

Al   That's what came into my head.

Bet   Well, thanks a lot.

Al   You wouldn't ever leave me, would you?

Bet   Why should I stay with you?

Al   Well, I love you.

Bet   You never say it.

Al   I've just said it.

Bet   I could kill you sometimes, you know.

Al   I know.

Bet   No Al, I mean really kill you. Put a pillow over your face while you're asleep, poison your coffee.

Al   Don't say that in here . . .

Bet   I know, but I've thought about it. I've thought about killing you.

Al   You haven't, you're only saying it.

Bet   I'm not. I have thought about it – about what would happen, but I never would.

Al   Is that because you love me?

Bet   No. I'm just scared of going to prison.

Pause.

Al   I don't want to go home. Do you?

Bet   No.

Al   There's nowt there. Let's stay here . . . We could live like tramps, walk around Paris, live off the land. I could get a job in Montmartre, painting.

Bet   Go steady.

Al   You don't think I'm any good, do you?

Bet   Well, you're not, are you?

Pause.

Al   There's nowt to go back for. Stay here and slowly work our way across Europe, finish up in China or somewhere,

then after a couple of years we could go back home.
Wouldn't it be brilliant? No ties, just eating the world up,
that'd be an education, wouldn't it?

Bet   I've always fancied going to India.

Al   Oooh, let's stay here, shall we? Let's bloody stay here!

Bet   Ssshhh!

*Suddenly we hear Jacques Brel's 'Ne Me Quitte Pas' loudly. The
atmosphere changes drastically. Paris is now a memory.*

Al *brings on the floor of their box.* **Bet** *brings on the chairs. The two
of them carry on the back wall. The practical hanging light is visible
again.*

Al *exits.*

Bet *sits and listens.*

Al *enters. Pause. The music fades.*

Al   Good tape, that. Glad we bought it.

Bet   Yeah, good tape. I can't understand a bloody word of
what he says. (*Pause.*) Oh well.

Al   Yeah.

Bet   I wonder where it all went.

Al   Ar.

Bet   Shall I play it again?

Al   No. We've been back a week and it's nearly worn out.

Pause.

Bet   Good laugh coming back, wasn't it?

Al   Yeah.

Bet   You did well, you only had one meal. And I wasn't
sick. Good crossing, wasn't it? I could go on them North Sea
Ferries all the time . . .

Pause.

Al   Do you want a coffee?

Bet   Oui . . . I'll have et coffee au lait.

Al   D'accord . . . Je having café noir.

Bet   Très bon. Avez vous una cuppa café noir?

Al   Oui, oui.

Bet   Bloody cold in here.

Al   No, hang on . . . I've got it. La chambre c'est frais.

Pause.

Bet   The room is a strawberry? I think you should throw that phrase book away.

Al   I just say owt, me . . . Shall I put the heating on?

Pause.

Bet   You and that duty free.

Al   Brilliant, int it?

Bet   All that wine. And chocolates.

Al   Brilliant.

Bet   And cigs, you bought five hundred cigs. We don't even smoke.

Al   I gave 'em to next door.

Bet   Five hundred cigs?

Al   Did you see me? I brought eight bottles of wine back.

Bet   You daft sod . . .

Al (*with a big sigh*)   Oh dear . . .

Bet   Yeah.

Al   I could eat sommat . . .

Bet   There's a plate of horse meat int kitchen.

Al   Lovely.

Bet   There's one of them croissants left if you want one.

Al   Can do.

Bet (*with a sigh*)   Shall we watch telly?

Al   Ophhhhh . . .

Bet   We could watch a video.

Al   A bloody video.

Bet   We had a good time, didn't we? (*Pause.*) Shall we play some records?

Al   I'm going to my shed.

Al *exits.*

Bet (*to herself*)   Oh dear . . .

Al *enters carrying a magazine. He is excited.*

Al   Here's one . . .

Bet   What is it?

Al   Here's one, I think we can do this one.

Bet   Okay, don't go manic, don't rush it.

Al   Ha ha . . . I think we can do this one.

Bet   Go on . . .

Al (*reading*)   'Say in not more than fifteen words why you would like to go to Mexico.'

Bet   Mexico.

Al   In not more than fifteen words.

Bet   Mexico.

Al   Go on then . . .

Bet What?

Al Say sommat . . .

Bet What's happened to that one about Euro Disney?

Al It's gone, it's int post. That wa' easy, I did that myself.
How many times a year should you change your
toothbrush, how many times a year should you brush your
teeth.

Bet It was for kids . . . Try and get sommat that rhymes,
that always impresses 'em.

Al Here you are, what about this? 'Mexico, Mexico, I
wanna go, to Mexico.'

Bet Why don't you leave it to me, let me do it?

Al All right then, know-all, here's one. 'Mexico is a
country full of spice, joy and culture with sand and sun and
many a vulture.'

Bet Do they have vultures in Mexico?

Al I don't know.

Bet You said that sun and sand bit about Florida.

Al I say the same in 'em all.

Bet And Greece.

Al It dun't matter . . .

Bet You've got no patience with 'em.

Al 'Mexico is a country that is spicy and hot . . . and I
want to go before I blow up . . .'

Bet Listen, just listen to me for a minute.

Al What?

Bet You're doing 'em every ten minutes. It took me three
weeks to do that one for Paris. Three weeks, sat looking
through, working sommat out, and then it's the luck of the

draw, it's a lottery . . . I mean, how much have you spent on them magazines? You can't move in that shed for magazines. We could save that money and go to Whitby or somewhere.

Al   What?

Bet   We could have a run on a bus somewhere.

Al   I'm not going to bloody Whitby.

Bet   It'd be a break.

Al   You go if you want, take Rita and Colin, they need a change of scenery.

Bet   It's somewhere to go for a little break.

Al   Bloody Whitby.

Bet   You can see Dracula's tomb. Bram Stoker and that.

Al   I'd rather hang myself.

Bet   There's an abbey.

Al   I want to go somewhere, I don't want to go up the road, do I? We might as well buy a tent and camp int garden.

Bet   Don't be daft, garden's not big enough.

Al   I don't want to stop, I want to go somewhere.

Bet   Oh, he's off.

Al   Do you want to stop here . . . look at it!

Bet   I should have pushed you off that bloody boat.

Al   Just bloody look at where we live!

Bet   Go on, shout. Let's hear what a big man you are.

Al   I'll call you sommat in a minute.

Bet   Go on, little boy, you can't do a quiz so you're throwing a tantrum.

Al   I said, didn't I? Once you've gone and had a look it's never the same. Once you've seen all that it's too much for your head.

Bet   Why?

Al   Because it's too bloody dangerous.

Bet   Is it heck.

Al   It is . . . it is . . .

Bet   What's dangerous about it apart from the Métro?

Al (*pointing to his head*)   All this up here, because you go and see all that and then you come back, and it doesn't fit somehow, it's not big enough, there's no room. And just think, we've only seen that much (*He holds up his thumb and index finger.*), we've only glanced at it . . .

Bet   At least we've been.

Al   You come back and listen to everybody go on and on about us being a part of Europe – which part are we? They must think everybody's bloody stupid here. We're not like them as far as I can see, we're a little island, and them that's got gets on, and them that's not gets shit on . . . and it's going to get worse.

Bet   There's probably people in France wi' no money, you know.

Al   I'm not thick.

Bet   We saw the best of it. I mean, there's probably people in France wi' nowt.

Pause.

Al   Well, at least they've got nice bread.

Bet   I bet some of 'em wished they lived here . . .

Al   I'll swap 'em.

Bet   It's just different, int it?

Al   We shouldn't'a been allowed to go to Paris, there ought to be a law against it. It's too bloody dangerous, we might start getting ideas. We might not want to watch 'Catchphrase' or 'Blind Date'.

Bet   You don't watch 'em anyway.

Al   We might start wanting sommat better.

Bet   Allus in that bloody shed.

Al   We might start wanting the pubs to open late, or cafés with good service or decent wages or painters in the streets, or buildings you can look at. We might just start wanting sommat more . . .

Bet   We've got buildings.

Al   What?

Bet   We've got beautiful buildings.

Al   Where . . . where . . . have we got owt decent?

Bet   York.

Al   Yeah, York, and that's it.

Bet   Edinburgh.

Al   You've never been.

Bet   I saw it ont Holiday Programme. Bath. Marina's nice in Hull.

Al   All right, I've heard you . . .

Bet   Beverley's nice, I think.

Al   All right . . . I get it.

Bet   Bolton Abbey . . . Castle Howard . . . down by the bridge is nice on a Sunday.

Al   All right, I get the point.

Bet   Aren't there any nice buildings in London?

Al It's all squashed up, int it, like everything here. You can't see it.

Bet France is bigger.

Al Thank you, Albert Einstein.

Bet (*musing*)   Int it funny, you have to go abroad to see what we've got here, I think. I wouldn't mind going to Windsor Castle one day.

Al Windsor Castle? There's nowt there – it's all been burnt!

Bet Or on one of them 'Whodunnit' weekends.

Al Whodunnit?

Bet There's nice buildings if you look. That's the trouble – we've never looked before, have we?

Al Bloody Whitby.

Bet Whitby'd be nice.

Al Whitby, who goes to Whitby?

Bet Or there's them Away Breaks. City break things. Gateshead. Seaburn.

Al Bloody Gateshead. Yippee! . . . Bloody Metro Centre . . .

Bet Captain Cook came from Whitby . . . be sommat to look at, nice coast line.

Pause.

Al (*sadly*)   Bloody Seaburn.

Bet Have you finished in there?

Al More or less.

Bet Well, go and get it then, let's have a look.

Al No . . . I'm not int mood.

Bet Go on, let's have a look at the new exhibition . . .

Al (*slowly leaving*)   Bloody Whitby, I could cry.

Al *exits*.

Bet *sits silently*.

Bet (*with a big sigh*)   Oh dear . . .

Al *enters with a canvas, much more colourful than the first, with a montage of Parisian places on it.* **Al** *holds it so that* **Bet** *can't see it.*

Al   Here you are . . . turn around . . . right. (*He holds up the painting.*)

Bet   Bloody hell, who's done that?

Al   Him next door.

Bet   It's brilliant.

Al   S'all right, int it?

Bet   I thought it was going to be another landscape.

Al   So did I.

Bet   We could sell that, get some cash.

Al   I'm not selling it, it's taken me ages to do it.

Bet   It's really good is that . . . Why are them others so awful?

Pause.

Al   It's a different style, int it?

Bet   It's Paris, int it?

Al   It looks all right, dun't it?

Pause.

Bet   Mmmmm.

Al   Anyway . . .

Bet   Yeah . . .

Al   Ah . . .

Bet   Yeah.

Al   Shall I make a coffee?

Bet   I'm not bothered.

Al   No? (*Pause.*) Yeah.

Bet   Ohhhmmmm.

Pause.

Al   Arrrmmmm.

Pause.

Bet   Oh dear . . .

Pause.

Al   'Hot as chilli, clear blue skies, Mexico is a big surprise.'

Music plays: 'La Bamba'.

The lights fade to blackout.

Perfect Pitch

Act One

Scene One

A caravan site. Day.

The east coast of Yorkshire. A large green plot of grass. A caravan is positioned on-stage. It has been cut away so that we can see inside. All the equipment for the caravan is new. **Ron**, *a middle aged, retired comprehensive school headmaster is attempting to push his van on to a pitch. It is a scorching summer's day. He wears sloppy clothes and a sun hat. Definitely not the outdoor type.* **Yvonne**, *his attractive wife, a few years younger, conducts the scene. Seagulls and crashing waves can be heard throughout.*

Yvonne Swing it!

Ron What?

Yvonne Swing it!

Ron I am!

Yvonne Pull it right round, it's not even straight. Come on, Ron, put your back into it.

Ron Is it moving?

Yvonne Swing it!

Ron Swing it? I'll swing you if you keep on.

Yvonne *finds this amusing.*

Yvonne You're a mile off the pitch, you should have come back a bit, the man said come back a few yards, I kept saying.

Ron (*a big effort*) Is that any better?

Yvonne Just swing it!

Ron (*another big effort*) Argh!

Music.

Blackout.

Scene Two

Minutes later.

Ron *has his arms under the front of the van and he is trying to force it sideways. It will not budge.*

Ron   It must be there now, surely?

Yvonne   No.

Ron   I can hear my heart racing.

Yvonne   It's not coming . . .

Ron   This is what the car's for, you know?

Yvonne   If you could back it and swing it, it would be perfect.

Ron   If I could back it and swing it, I'd be in the bloody Olympics.

Yvonne   It's not even moving.

Ron   Something is. I think I've pulled my stomach.

Yvonne   Try and rock it.

Ron   Rock it?

Yvonne   You're nearly there.

Ron   You're the fitness freak, you should be doing this.

Ron *gives in exhausted.*

Is that any better?

Yvonne   I kept saying left.

Ron   I kept turning left.

Yvonne   No you turned right when I said left. I said left but you turned right. I said left hand down.

Ron   When I put my left hand down, Yvonne, I went right.

Yvonne   Well I did say left.

Ron (*breathless*)   Never mind what you said, is that any good?

Music.

Blackout.

Scene Three

Twenty minutes later.

Ron *stands looking at the caravan.* **Yvonne** *looks across the pitch. She is concerned.*

Yvonne   I don't know if I wouldn't prefer it over there.

Ron   You can park the damn thing next time.

Yvonne   I thought it was going to go over the cliff!

Ron   It nearly did.

Yvonne   Why are you so useless at practical things?

Ron   I felt such a pillock, was everybody watching?

Yvonne   Not everyone. Just the site warden!

Ron   I bet he can spot first-timers a mile off.

Yvonne   I said you'd dropped it too short, but you wouldn't listen.

Ron *surveys the location.*

Ron   So this is it? Cliff Top Caravan Site? Well one thing's for sure, it's on a cliff top!

Yvonne   Shall we get the gas on?

Ron   It looks like a quiet site anyway.

Yvonne   All the recommended ones were fully booked. I just looked in the *Yellow Pages* and phoned up.

Ron   At least we're away from everyone else.

Yvonne   Thank God! They'll not be able to see you making a fool of yourself.

Ron   Exactly!

Ron *holds his stomach.*

Do you know, I think I've ruptured myself towing that about, to be honest. I've ripped all across my stomach.

Yvonne   Do you think we'll be all right here?

Ron   Well I'm not towing it about any more.

Yvonne   No, I mean on this site?

Ron   Why shouldn't we?

Yvonne   Well it's not exactly La Rochelle is it?

Ron   I thought we'd agreed on this?

Yvonne   You agreed.

Ron   You agreed as well.

Yvonne   A trial run, I said.

Ron   This is a trial run.

Yvonne   I thought we'd go in the back field, and then have our first real go in France.

Ron   What sense would there have been putting it on the back field, that's where we park it?

Yvonne   Well it would have been just enough.

Ron   No, we're better off coming up here.

Yvonne   I think it's so down-market though.

Ron   It's all right, it's perfect. Nobody to bother us.

A beat.

Yvonne   I mean Claire and Barry bought a gîte with his redundancy money and look what we got?

Ron   Well you can't tour in a gîte! You can try, but it's a hard tow.

Yvonne   And he wasn't even the head of school, was he?

Ron   Why are you worried about what Claire and Barry do?

Yvonne   Well they always thought they were better than us.

Ron   So what?

Yvonne   Well they will be now! I don't even know why you had to tell anyone we'd bought one.

Ron   Well it's a bit difficult to hide, isn't it? Especially when it's stuck to the back of your bloody car!

Yvonne   They only came round to gloat.

Ron *looks at the pitch.*

Ron   I'll get the awning, shall I? Where is it?

Yvonne   It's still in the car.

Ron   Oh hell . . . I thought we'd unpacked it.

Ron *turns to depart.*

Yvonne   I told you not to park all the way down there.

Ron   I didn't have much choice, did I? The warden told me not to park on the edge. You know what this coast's like, too much weight and we're in the sea. I'll probably cripple myself carrying it all the way up here but . . .

Ron *sets off to exit.*

Yvonne   Go get 'em, Tiger!

Ron   It's supposed to be a relaxing weekend. I've ruptured myself and lost three stone, and we've only been here twenty minutes.

Ron *exits.*

Music.

Blackout.

Scene Four

Fifteen minutes later.

Yvonne *is caught in motion as she sorts out tables and chairs.* **Ron** *enters carrying a large awning sack and a few metal pegs and a hammer. He begins to sort out the awning and is speaking throughout his work.*

Ron   Don't bother putting anything in the car on the way back, I'll carry everything, might as well.

Yvonne   We've been lucky to get a pitch this far out when you think about it. I suppose I'm quite looking forward to it really.

Ron   I'm not looking forward to putting this up. Where are the instructions?

Yvonne   I've not seen them.

Ron   Well I haven't.

Yvonne   Well do you need 'em?

Ron   Well I might.

Yvonne   Well where are they?

Ron   Well I don't know. I put them somewhere safe.

Yvonne   Where?

Ron   If I knew where . . .

Yvonne   Can't you try and put it up without?

Ron   Well I can try.

Yvonne   Well try that then.

Ron   Yeh, because it looks so easy, doesn't it? It looks like a piece of cake.

Yvonne   It can't be that bad, everyone else has got theirs up.

Ron *takes the awning and its metal bits from its bag.*

Ron   No bloody instructions! It'll probably be time for home before I get it up.

Yvonne   Do you want a hand?

Ron   No, you just stand there taking in the view, I'll see to it. I'll see to it if it kills me. Look at this lot!

Yvonne   You'll enjoy it when everything's ready . . .

Ron   When everything's ready it'll be dark.

Yvonne (*still looking at the coastline*)   This is a great coastline. You can follow the length of the coast all along here, look. That's one good thing, I'll be able to get some runs in.

Ron   You should try doing this if you want to keep fit. This is how they should train for the London Marathon, caravan pulling, and awning erecting, it's all cardio-vascular work, Sally Gunnell recommends it apparently.

Yvonne   You know I'd forgotten how beautiful it is up here. I haven't been to Scarborough since I was about seven. Mind you, all we did then was play bingo and eat fish and chips. I suppose it's good for the soul, back to nature and all that.

Ron   Oh you!

Yvonne   What?

Ron *is holding a number of pieces of string and metal.*

Ron   It's hardly back to nature, is it? We've got a full electricity supply, gas central heating, and a toilet. We haven't even got that at home! I mean the car boot's full of food from Marks and plastic stuff from Betaware. We've not exactly come to camp out in a hole and eat rabbits, have we?

Yvonne   Well I haven't!

Ron   Mind you, I don't think I'm going to be able to take advantage of the toilet anyway.

Yvonne   Why not?

Ron   I can't fit my legs in.

Yvonne   They say it's only for use in emergencies, anyway.

Ron   It will be an emergency if I get in there, you'd have to call the fire brigade to get me out. Now is that the back or the front?

Music.

Blackout.

Scene Five

Five minutes later.

Ron *is still struggling with the awning, it is all out over the pitch.*
Yvonne *is looking at the sea view.*

Yvonne   It looks like a nice run along that cliff edge.

Ron   That's good then.

Yvonne   You should try it, you need some exercise.

Ron   No I'm fine, honestly.

Ron *is now completely under the awning holding two metal sticks.*
Yvonne *walks to pick up some packaging and takes them into the*

caravan and begins to unpack. **Ron** *plays the entire scene from under the awning.*

Yvonne   I think I'm beginning to unwind already. Are you?

Ron   Completely.

Yvonne   It's not too bad for space, you know? Cosy I think.

Ron   How the bloody hell . . . ?

Ron *still struggles.*

You couldn't just give us a hand?

Yvonne   Sorry, love. I'm unpacking.

Music.

Blackout.

Scene Six

Five minutes later.

Lights come up and **Ron** *is still under the awning. He is having no luck at all.* **Yvonne** *stands watching.*

Ron   It just doesn't make sense.

Yvonne   The man I bought it off was sixty-nine and had been caravanning all his life.

Ron   And not once had he managed to get the awning up. Not in sixty-nine years. (*Easily.*) This bastard, bastard thing.

Yvonne   What's the problem?

Ron   The instructions, we're lost without them, that's the problem.

Yvonne   Well don't lose your temper, they can hear you all over the site. We don't want to get thrown off, do we?

Ron   We'll probably get thrown off for not putting the awning up, I think it's some kind of initiation ceremony.

Yvonne   Do you want to leave it?

Ron   Well if we could possibly live without it I'd be grateful. There is no way this is going up without the instructions.

Yvonne   Well I've said leave it. I don't know why you have to keep going on about it. Throw it out of the way and just leave it. Don't let's have a scene.

Ron *picks up the awning and deposits it under the caravan.*

Ron   Well I've passed the caravan parking, and failed the awning erecting miserably.

Yvonne   You only just scraped a pass at caravan parking though, didn't you?

Ron   Yes, the story of my life.

Music.

Blackout.

Scene Seven

An hour later.

Yvonne *lays out a few bits of picnic-type food.* **Ron** *is looking around the pitch, he takes in all the stage.* **Yvonne** *has a bottle of wine.*

Ron   Where did you say you were going to run to, then?

Yvonne   Right down the coast.

Ron   To Folkestone?

Yvonne   Do you want wine?

Ron   I'll just have a can of beer. You have one if you want!

Yvonne *takes the wine into the caravan.* **Ron** *gets a can of beer and pours it deliberately into a small glass.*

Yvonne   Not for me.

Ron   I don't know, three months without a drink?

Yvonne   That's good.

Ron   That is good. I'm not complaining. It's the act of a saint as far as I'm concerned. If I get through one night, I've done rather well.

They sit and relax. Things aren't so bad after all. **Yvonne** *gets a script from the caravan and begins to study it.*

Ron   Mmm.

Yvonne   Mmmm.

Ron   Yes, not bad at all.

Yvonne   That's us sorted then.

Ron   How's that going?

Yvonne   Fine.

Ron   What is it, *Pinafore*?

Yvonne   *Mikado*!

Ron   Who's doing it this time, is it Peter?

Yvonne   George Moonie.

Ron   He's tone deaf.

Yvonne   He's not.

Ron   He was tone deaf when he taught in the science department twenty years ago, and I bet he hasn't got much better.

Yvonne   You should've stayed with the amateur dramatics, it would have given you something to do.

Ron   I've got something to do. I'm going to learn how to put an awning up. That should take me at least two years.

Yvonne   You used to enjoy it, didn't you?

Ron   Yes, but I got fed up of the same old arguments. Can you remember? Endless discussions about whether Peter should call himself director or producer? And when he eventually got the show on it was just an excuse for a sly snog at the after show party and a cup of champagne from a plastic cup.

Yvonne   Oh you make it sound awful.

Ron   It is usually.

Yvonne   We're not that bad.

Ron   You're not, but look at the others. Look at Barbara Scott!

Yvonne   She used to be a professional.

Ron   A professional what?

Yvonne   They reckon she sang with a band.

Ron   I don't think she was there for the singing.

Yvonne   Ron?

Ron   Well!

Yvonne   I mean her husband had left her for another man, that must have been crippling.

Ron   Who for?

Yvonne   I mean, what does that say about her?

Ron   When we did *Guys and Dolls* she used to trap me in the corner of the wings. She was all over me. Talk about getting stage fright? I got wings fright with Barbara Scott. That's probably why her husband left her, she scared him to death. Living with a Kiwi front row would be heaven compared to living with Barbara. I bet she weighed fifty stone.

Yvonne   You were such a good Big Julie though.

A beat.

Ron   Not as good as she would've been.

Music.

Blackout.

Scene Eight

Evening.

In the blackout a caravan awning has been erected off stage and a large old caravan has appeared. **Ron** *looks at it in exasperation.* **Yvonne** *enters. She has been for a walk.*

Yvonne   Can you believe the weather?

Ron   Look at this!

Yvonne   I've just walked as far as Filey. It's lovely, isn't it?

Ron   It would be if he hadn't pitched that there.

Yvonne   Oh right!

Ron   All this space and he has to park it there.

Yvonne   Who is it?

Ron   God only knows. I fell asleep and when I woke up again there they were, awning up and every damn thing.

Yvonne   There was a bit of a climb coming back.

Ron   All this space.

Yvonne *begins to take off her trainers.*

Yvonne   Yes, that's going to be a nice run in the mornings. Right on the cliff top.

Ron   Awning up and everything.

Yvonne   What did you say?

Ron   Must have got that awning up in no time. Mind you, it's not like that one of ours, is it?

Yvonne   Did you see them?

Ron   I haven't seen a soul.

Yvonne   Well they're not affecting us, are they?

Ron   All the space on this edge and somebody has to park there.

Yvonne   Maybe they wanted the view as well.

Ron   I don't like them being that near!

Yvonne   That's what happens on caravan sites, other people pull up at the side of you and you start to have conversations, that's why people go away, they don't want to stay in their back garden completely hidden from the world. It's called society, Ron. That's why I wanted to go to France, at least there was a chance of meeting somebody different.

Ron   Different to what?

Yvonne   To the bloody English!

Ron   Oh we're off.

Yvonne   Well . . . !

Yvonne *sits.* **Ron** *has another can of beer.*

Ron   Oh well, there's not a lot we can do, is there? Can I tempt you?

Yvonne   Three months and two days since my last one.

Ron   Twenty minutes, and three seconds since mine.

Yvonne   Put a tape on?

Ron   Absolutely!

Yvonne *finds a tape and cassette player.*

Yvonne   A little bit of ambience.

Ron   What have you got?

Yvonne   Classic experience.

Ron   Which?

Yvonne   Nocturne!

Ron   What else!

Yvonne   A little adagio and we'll be well away . . .

Ron   It's beautiful here, I'll tell you that.

Yvonne   I love this.

They slip on a classic experience cassette. They sit as Debussey 'Clare de Lune' plays.

Ron   Oh yes.

Yvonne   I take it all back.

Ron   Not bad so far, the old caravanning.

Yvonne   No I'll give you that. I love this peace.

Ron   Oh dear!

Yvonne   Lovely!

Ron   Mmm.

Yvonne   Very nice.

Ron   Very.

Yvonne   Very very nice.

They begin to hum and conduct the music. As they do this we hear love-making coming from inside the other caravan. It is very vocal and excitable. It is the voice of a coarse young northern woman.

Steph   Oh, oh . . . oh, oh, oh, oh.

Ron   This is a very good recording.

Yvonne   It is actually.

Ron   To say it's tape.

Yvonne   Very good to say it's tape, isn't it?

Ron   I think it's one of those digitally re-mastered jobs.

Yvonne   I don't mind tape really . . .

Steph   Oh, oh, oh, oh, oh.

Ron *tries to listen to the music but he can hear* **Steph**'s *moans too.*

Ron   What's that?

Yvonne   What?

Ron   That . . .

Yvonne   What?

Ron   Turn it down a bit.

They turn down the radio cassette. And we can now hear the love-making very clearly.

Steph   Oh! Oh! Oh!

Ron   That!

Yvonne   Oh well.

Ron   Oh right!

Yvonne   Mmmm!

Ron *gets up to go and look off stage.*

Yvonne   Where are you going?

Ron   For a look.

Yvonne   Ron!

Ron   Look at that!

Yvonne   What?

Ron   Amazing, the whole bloody caravan's rocking.

Yvonne   Come away.

Steph   Oh, oh, oh, oh, oh.

Ron *is transfixed looking at the other caravan.*

Ron   Nobody makes that sort of noise, do they?

Yvonne   We did.

Ron   You're joking aren't you?

Yvonne   We did.

Ron   Yvonne, we used to do it at my mother's and didn't even make a sound, you know how light a sleeper my mum is. I was holding my breath some of the time. It's a wonder I didn't die.

Steph   Oooooooh!

Ron   That is just . . .

Yvonne   Wonderful, by the sound of it.

Ron   The whole sodding van is moving. If they're not careful it'll be over the edge.

Ron *comes back to* **Yvonne**.

And what are you grinning at?

Yvonne   What?

Ron   You, you're grinning.

Yvonne   I am not.

Ron   You've got a right grin on your bloody face.

Yvonne   I haven't.

Ron   You're positively glowing.

Yvonne   That's the fresh air.

Steph   Oh, oh, oh . . .

Ron   That's pollution that is!

Steph   Don't stop, don't stop, yes, oh!

Yvonne   You're the one who's grinning.

Ron   I'm not.

Yvonne   You are.

Steph   Oh, oh, oh, oh!!

Ron   This is insane. (*Shouts.*) Pack it in! Turn the radio up.

Yvonne   Don't you think it reminds you of the good old days.

Ron   What, the television programme?

Yvonne   Don't be daft.

A beat.

Ron   We've never made a noise like that, never ever.

Yvonne   Oh we have.

Ron   We haven't.

Yvonne   What about when we went to stay at Jeff and Margi's?

Ron   I'd only just met you!

Yvonne   Well maybe he's just met her?

Ron   I had to make a lot of noise to cover the sound of my chest wheezing. I got asthma!

Yvonne   Another romantic night.

Ron   Maybe it's two women.

Yvonne   Maybe it's two men? Maybe it's Barbara Scott's husband? Sounds like they're having a good time whoever it is!

Ron   Turn the radio up a bit, it's making me feel sick.

Yvonne   Oh sometimes!

Steph   Oh, oh, oh, oh!

Ron   No honestly. That is sickening.

Yvonne   It isn't.

Ron   I mean what are they doing?

Yvonne   Just put your mind off it.

Ron   Easier said than done.

Yvonne   It's only natural.

Ron   It doesn't sound it!

Steph   Oh, oh yes oh, yes!

A beat.

Ron   I have never made a woman moan like that.

Yvonne   I'm trying to learn this. (*Mikado* book.)

Ron   Except at college. I was noisy at college.

Yvonne   Oh here we go.

Steph   Oh, oh, oh, yes . . .

Ron   The trouble was it was me who made all the noise. I was with this girl once . . .

Yvonne   Spare me the details.

Steph   Oh, oh, oh yes, oh . . .

Ron   I was moaning like hell, because I'd got my feet caught in the end of the bed!

Steph   Yes, yes, yes.

Ron   I always made all the noise, come to think of it.

Steph   Yes, yes. Arghhh!

Silence.

Ron   Well that's that then.

Yvonne   You can relax now?

A beat.

Ron   They must be knackered.

Yvonne   Beats jogging so they say.

Ron   They must be absolutely bloody shattered.

Ron *gets up and saunters over to the caravan.*

Yvonne   Come away.

Ron   You can't keep that up for that length of time without it taking its toll on your health, surely.

Yvonne   Well it's obviously new to them, whoever it is.

Ron *saunters back to base.*

Ron   You never ever made much of a noise, did you?

Yvonne   Meaning?

Ron   I was just thinking.

Yvonne   Leave it.

Ron   Thank God they've finished anyway.

Yvonne   You never know, we might be doing the same!

Ron   Oh yes?

Yvonne   Never know your luck.

Ron   I don't think so. I can't fit in the bed for a start.

Yvonne   How do you know?

Ron   Because I tried when you went for a walk. I put the whole bed down. If I sleep straight out I'll end up with a flat head and if I slept on my side I'll be like Quasimodo in the morning.

Silence.

Steph   Oh, oh, oh, oh, oh, oh . . .

Ron   Not again! Please not again!

Steph   Oh, oh, oh, yes, oh.

Ron   Oh come on this is ridiculous!

Music.

Blackout.

Scene Nine

Half an hour later.

Silence. **Ron** *is in the caravan.* **Yvonne** *is outside. Both are packing away their bits and bobs.* **Steph** *enters. She is a rough looking girl in her mid-twenties who smokes. She speaks in a coarse northern brogue.*

Ron   I don't know how they even managed it, to be honest.

Yvonne   What?

Ron   You can't swing a cat in here!

Yvonne   You can put the beds down in a minute.

Ron   I think that there might be a bottleneck for the sink, every time I turn around, I bang my knees or something.

Steph *enters from her caravan.*

Steph   Bloody hell, warm tonight, int it?

Yvonne   Sorry?

Steph   I say, a nice night!

Yvonne   Lovely.

Steph   Yeh.

Yvonne   Warm!

Steph   Bloody boiling, int it?

Yvonne   It is, isn't it?

A beat.

Yvonne   Nice site.

Steph   You been before?

Yvonne   No, this is our first time.

Steph   New van!

Yvonne   Yes.

Steph   Look at ours. Dropping to bits. Looks good yours.

Yvonne   Oh thanks.

Steph   Three hundred quid off Grant's brother, ours.

Yvonne   Well Ron's just taken early retirement from teaching so we . . .

Steph   No, it's not bad up here.

Yvonne   So we thought . . .

Steph   This site's a bit dull, but at least it's cheap.

Yvonne   Give it a go you know, thought about it and . . .

Steph   We come up a lot. I like to do the clubs. Grant dun't like leaving the dogs but . . .

Yvonne   Ever so nice, the coast.

Ron *enters from the caravan.*

Oh this is Ron. This is?

Steph   Steph.

Ron   Oh right?

Steph   Are you all right then?

Ron   Yes.

Steph   That's all right then.

Ron   Yeas, I'm fine.

Silence.

Yvonne   Just saying, Steph comes up here a lot.

Ron   Really?

Yvonne   She says the site's a bit dull though.

Ron (*dead*)   Oh I wouldn't say that, it's been very interesting so far.

Steph   You have to make your own entertainment.

Ron   So I gather.

Steph   There's a club on the site next door, if you're into karaoke and that.

Ron   One for you, Yvonne.

Yvonne   You never know.

Steph   Eh?

Ron   Yvonne sings.

Steph   Oh right then!

Yvonne   Well, you know . . .

Ron   Gilbert and Sullivan.

Steph   Oh hell . . .

Ron   She's good actually . . .

A beat.

Steph   Anyway. Just go for a shower. It gets a bit sweaty inside in this weather.

Ron   That's right.

Steph   There's quite a lot going off in town, you know, if you . . .

Ron   That's right . . .

Steph   Anyway, see you later . . .

Steph *strides towards the shower block.*

Ron   Mmm.

Yvonne   Well.

Ron   Difficult to know what to say.

Yvonne   I could see that.

Ron   Well what are you supposed to say? How was it for you? I can't wait to see what the other half is like.

Yvonne   Oh please!

Ron   You mean you're not interested?

As they sit, **Grant** *ambles on to stage. He is a man the same age as* **Ron** *but distinctly rounded, aggressive and dirty. He wears a vest, some dirty tracksuit bottoms, and is sweating. He is frightening.*

Grant   Huh!

Yvonne   Evening.

Grant   Huh.

Grant *exits.*

Yvonne   So there!

Ron   He's your man.

Yvonne   Talkative.

Ron   He's obviously breathless, the poor sod. I'm going to see what he has for his breakfast. Whatever he has, I'll have two of.

Yvonne   He must be at least your age.

Ron   I wondered what those tyres hanging from trees were for when we came in. Now I know.

Yvonne   Really?

Ron   They're obviously for him to swing on.

Music.

Blackout.

Scene Ten

The next morning.

Yvonne *is tidying up the remains of last night's snack.* **Steph** *enters. She puts up a couple of chairs outside her awning.*

Steph   I tell you sommat, I feel like shit this morning.

Yvonne   Really?

Steph   Didn't get back till gone two!

Yvonne   I was up at six. Just me on the sands. Well, me and a dog, jogging . . . You okay?

Steph   I've got such a head!

Yvonne   Oh dear.

Steph   I was mixing it. We went down to the Nelson.

Yvonne   I've got some tablets if you . . .

Steph (*lighting a cigarette*)   No, one of these and I'll be sorted.

A beat.

You say you've been running?

Yvonne   Just sorting out a course.

Steph   What for?

Yvonne   I want to do next year's marathon.

Steph   Oh hell!

Yvonne   That's what I'm beginning to think.

Steph   Run for a bus and I'm knackered. I keep saying I'm gunna give up these but . . .

Yvonne   Oh you'd get into it if you put your mind to it.

A beat.

Steph   You sleep all right then?

Yvonne   Not bad thanks, but it's not really my thing, I'm afraid. I'm making the best of a bad job really.

Steph   Why's that? It's a lovely van, I wish we'd got one like it.

Yvonne   Well . . . it's okay but . . .

Steph   Swap you!

Yvonne   I don't think Ron'd be keen, it's become his pride and joy.

Steph   What's up then?

Yvonne   Well nothing. Not a lot to do though!

Steph   There's some good shops in Scarborough. There's a Pizza Hut and all if you fancy.

Yvonne   Well, it's not that so much . . .

Steph   What then?

Yvonne   We were going to France but Ron changed his mind at the last minute.

Steph   Oh right. I've only ever been to Calais.

Yvonne   Oh it's nice, isn't it?

Steph   Didn't see much of it, we just went to a supermarket and then we came straight back. Nine hours, there and back!

Yvonne   Really!

Steph   Yeh. Grant doesn't like being away from the dogs.

Yvonne   Have you got kennels?

Steph   Just in the garden, he breeds bull terriers.

Yvonne   Oh right.

Steph   He's dog mad. He's on about seeing some of his dog mates on Saturday so I says I'm going down town then.

Yvonne   Good for you!

Steph   Well, I'm not going to sit and listen to them bore each other senseless. And I don't fancy staying here by myself so . . .

Yvonne   You're having a night on the town then?

Steph   Hey don't knock it!

Yvonne   I wasn't.

Steph   Yeh, I thought I'd sample the nightlife.

Yvonne   Good for you!

Steph   Dead right!

A beat.

Yvonne   Well I don't know what we're doing this weekend yet!

Steph   You can come out with me if you want?

Yvonne   What?

Steph   You can come down town with me!

Yvonne   Oh right.

Steph   Do you want?

Yvonne   Well . . .

Steph   I'm only going to have a pizza or sommat.

Yvonne   Oh really?

Steph   If you fancy a change.

Yvonne   Well I think Ron might not . . .

Steph   I mean, might even see if there's a show on or sommat, I usually go and see sommat.

Yvonne   Take advantage!

Steph   Have you seen the Grumbleweeds, they might be on?

Yvonne   I have actually . . .

Steph   There must be sommat on at the Futurist?

Yvonne   I suppose so.

Steph   I'll have a look, shall I?

Yvonne   Well yes I suppose there must be something on, it's high season, isn't it?

Steph   I'm going into Scarborough, I can get some tickets if you want?

Yvonne   Well I . . .

Steph   Please yourself!

Yvonne   Well . . . ?

Steph   I mean, I'm not forcing you. It's just that he dun't like me going down town on my own.

Yvonne   No, right.

Steph   Anyway!

Yvonne   No, no that's fine, I'll come for a pizza.

Steph   Yeh?

Yvonne   Ron'll just have to sit and read. Hang on.

Steph   What?

Yvonne   Actually I think I've got a leaflet for the Futurist. Shall I have a look?

Yvonne *goes towards the caravan.*

Steph (*shouts*)   I'm not into Gilbert O Sullivan or opera or owt, so!

Yvonne   Hang on. I picked one up with a load of other stuff. Hang on. I got some when we first arrived. I always do, I always get a handful of leaflets. I just grab them from the tourist place, do you?

Yvonne *goes into the caravan and pulls out a leaflet for the Futurist Theatre.*

Here we are. Let's have a look. Roy Chubby Brown.

Steph   Oh I've seen him, he's brilliant!

Yvonne   Is he really?

Steph   Funny.

Yvonne   Let's have a look! No, I don't think there's anything. Oh Tommy Steele, oh we've missed him! Oh that's a shame, I would have fancied that. I like him! Let's have a look. Steve Coogan, gone! Ah Saturday! One night only, 'The Ultimate Female Fantasy'. Ladies only. No I don't think that's for us . . . do you?

Steph   What is it?

Yvonne   A strip act, that's not what we're after, is it?

Steph   Why not?

Yvonne   Well . . .

Steph   Should be a laugh. I've always wanted to see one.

Yvonne   Well I don't think it's for me!

Steph   Why not?

Yvonne   No, not for me . . .

A beat.

Steph   Can I have a look at that.

Steph *looks at the leaflet.*

Oh yeh. A female fantasy show! Hey they look good on the poster anyway.

Yvonne   Yes, but is it art?

Steph   No, but I bet it's a laugh.

Yvonne   Do you think so?

Steph   Don't you fancy it?

Yvonne   Are you joking?

Steph   I bet it's great.

Yvonne   What about, erm . . . ?

Steph   Oh he'll not be bothered . . .

Yvonne   Oh!

Steph   What's up, won't he like you going?

Yvonne   It's not that . . .

Steph   I mean, it's only a bit of fun, isn't it?

Yvonne   I don't think it's me though.

Steph   If you don't want to come . . .

A beat.

Yvonne   I'd better forget about it actually.

Steph   Well, please yourself, but they've got nothing that you haven't seen before, have they?

Yvonne   Who knows?

Steph   Well, think about it.

Yvonne   I don't . . .

Steph   We'll just have sommat to eat then. I mean, I can't go on my own anyway, can I? Not to sommat like that, I mean what do you think I am, a pervert?

Steph *exits as* **Ron** *comes from the washroom.*

Ron   Bloody hay fever. I thought the sea air might sort it out but it obviously hasn't. What's it like down there?

Yvonne Wonderful on the sands. I'm going to do a three mile jog in the morning and a ten mile run in the afternoon.

Ron I tried to phone the firm by the way. The man said, get some two by one and fix it yourself. I nearly went ballistic. All that money and he said fix it yourself! What are you doing, planning an outing?

Yvonne Just seeing what was on in Scarborough. She's invited me out for a pizza.

Ron Well that's nice of her! They're not too bad, are they?

Yvonne Is the washroom busy?

Ron No, no it's quiet, and it's clean, if you get there in the morning it's spotless. Fix it yourself, he said. A brand new caravan and the bloody bed breaks. I wouldn't mind but we weren't doing anything!

Yvonne I'll pop and get myself sorted then.

Yvonne *jogs off.* **Ron** *sits and looks at a paper he has with him. As he does* **Grant** *comes from the caravan.*

Ron Morning.

Grant Huh.

Ron All well.

Grant Eh?

Ron What?

Grant Eh?

Ron Nothing.

Grant Oh.

Ron Only morning.

Grant Oh.

Ron That's all.

Grant Thee brake's not on.

Ron I beg your pardon!

Grant *goes near to* **Ron***'s van and inspects it.*

Grant Thee brake's not on. It's a wonder thy ant run backwards during the night.

Ron Oh shit, that's the brake is it?

Grant And tha wants to put that waste tank on its side, it'll be better like that.

Ron Oh right. It didn't say on the instructions.

Grant And get some bits of wood and put them under your supports, otherwise you'll ruin the pitch for somebody else.

Ron Oh right, yes!

Grant Then you can get more purchase.

Ron Thanks for that.

Grant Tha's not been int van before then?

Ron No, no!

Grant No, I thought not!

Birds twitter. **Ron** *watches him go. And goes to change the waste tank.*

Music.

Blackout.

Scene Eleven

Later that day.

Yvonne *is coming back from her shower and fixes up a small washing line. She hangs her smalls on a small line. She is wearing hot*

pants, looks flushed and radiant. She has recently finished a long run.
Grant *comes to her, and watches her.* **Yvonne** *sings to herself.*

Yvonne   Hiya. Gave me a shock. You okay. Nice day.
Ron's just gone for the phone, he can't get a signal here, he
likes to phone the girls, see how things are at home. Is there
anything wrong?

Grant   I was just seeing if he'd seen to that waste tank.

Yvonne   Oh right.

Grant   He'd got it the wrong way up.

Yvonne   Yes, he's not the best in the world at outdoor
things. He thinks he is, but . . .

Grant   He'll learn.

Yvonne   Lovely today again, isn't it?

A beat.

Grant   So she says you're going to see some strippers or
sommat?

Yvonne   Well actually . . .

Grant   Ah, you buggers!

Yvonne   I'm not sure yet.

Grant   That's what she said.

Yvonne   Maybe.

Grant   Well you'd better tell her.

Yvonne   Oh right.

Grant   You seen 'em before?

Yvonne   No.

Grant   I bet she wets hersen, she gets that excited over
owt like that.

Yvonne   Really?

Grant   Load of bollocks to me, but . . .

Ron *enters on the end of this line.*

Ron   Couldn't get through, I had to walk right to the site office and ring from a land line. Just been to phone the girls. We've got three. Daughters. Girls, well, little women now!

Grant   I was just checking your waste tank, see if you'd done it.

Ron   Not yet.

Grant   Get it done, man, do the job right!

Ron   Yes, I had to walk all the way down there to make a bloody phone call. Got this mobile, useless half the time aren't . . .

Grant   . . . I was just saying, you'd better be on your guard when they've been down to watch them strippers. They might come back with some right ideas.

Grant *exits.*

Ron   What's all that about?

Yvonne   She asked me if I wanted to go for a pizza. I said yes, and now she's gone and got some tickets for a male strip show.

Ron   Oh nice.

Yvonne   I told her not to bother.

Ron   Why don't you go another night, to see something decent?

Yvonne   It's Roy Chubby Brown! We've just missed Tommy Steele.

Ron   Well tell her you don't want to go . . .

Yvonne   I did! But Grant's going out with some mates and she'll be going around town on her own.

Ron   Oh right!

Yvonne   Well it doesn't seem right, does it?

Ron   I thought you hated all that stuff?

Yvonne   Well I don't know, do I? I've never been, have I?

Ron   So I'll be sat reading David Lodge and you're going to be watching an officer and a gentleman get his kit off!

Yvonne   Sounds like you know all about it?

Ron   Some of the science department went to something like it!

Yvonne   And?

Ron   Well, they said it was a disappointment actually! Except for Pauline West, she loved it. She went back the next night I think. But you know Pauline, she can't get enough of it! Well I'd better see to this bloody waste tank before he beats me up.

Ron *puts the waste tank on its side, then calls across to* **Grant**.

I've done it!

Blackout.

Scene Twelve

Evening, later.

Ron, **Yvonne**, **Steph** *and* **Grant** *are sat around the small plastic table.* **Steph** *smokes heavily.* **Grant** *has a can of beer. Things are unnecessarily friendly between them. We should get the impression that this conversation has been going on some time.*

Yvonne   You'll not believe this, so anyway when we eventually got to bed Ron turned over and the bed split in half.

Ron   It did. Snap!

Yvonne   I thought his back had gone.

Ron　I thought it was my stomach.

Yvonne　He phoned them up, didn't you?

Ron　I phoned them up, this morning.

Yvonne　The man at the firm said, just get a bit of wood . . .

Ron　Fourteen thousand quid. Cash.

Steph　Cash?

Yvonne　The man said just get a piece of two by one . . .

Ron　. . . Two by one he said.

Yvonne　And mend it yourself.

Steph　Mend it yourself?

Yvonne　I thought, 'Ron mend anything, he's no good at anything practical, intellectual yes, but practical things no way.'

Steph　What were you doing to break the bed?

Ron　Just rolling over?

Steph　Argh?

Yvonne　He's no good at all with his hands.

Steph　Not very good with your hands then?

Ron　I can put a shelf up.

Yvonne　If pushed.

Steph　Grant does all our stuff, don't you?

No reply.

He does all our stuff.

Yvonne　No, not with Ron, if we're having any decorating done we have to get somebody in. And I don't understand why, because his father was a painter on the council, wasn't he?

Grant   Have you seen the gob on her?

Silence.

Yvonne   I'm sorry?

Grant   Your gob, it's non stop, int it?

Yvonne   What about it?

Grant   She's got a right gob on her, ant she, like a bloody opera singer or sommat! I mean she's got like a singer's mouth, ant she?

Ron   She's got perfect pitch, haven't you?

Grant   Oh aye. What do you sing then?

Yvonne   All sorts.

Ron   She read music at Oxford.

Yvonne   She?

Ron   Sorry.

Grant   Sing sommat then?

Yvonne   Not here.

Grant   I bet she's shit, aren't you?

Ron   We went on a cruise last year, and she won a talent contest, didn't you?

Yvonne   I'm not singing here, Ron.

Steph   I wouldn't mind going on a cruise.

Grant   Well you've had that.

All laugh.

Ron   And us, we're not going on another one.

Yvonne   It cost us a fortune . . .

Grant   You pay that in cash?

Ron   It's not bad, you know, a cruise, they've got all the stuff.

Grant   It's the people though, int it?

Ron   Well?

Steph   They're all a bit . . .

Ron   Well, we weren't.

Grant   Yeh, she's got a good mouth ant she? I thought when I saw her, I thought, she's got a singer's mouth that woman.

Steph   He won't stop in a hotel.

Yvonne   No?

Steph   He hates hotels, don't you?

Grant *suddenly rises.*

Grant   Right come on then!

Steph   Are we going?

Grant   Go and have a walk, and have some fish and chips. Do you want owt fetching?

Ron   No I . . . ?

Yvonne   We're fine thanks.

Grant   Right come on.

Grant *moves off.* **Steph** *lingers.*

Steph   Don't forget to get your ticket off me . . .

Grant   Aye she dun't want you changing your mind and her havin' to go herself! Come on!

Steph   I'm comin'.

Steph *walks over to* **Grant** *and they walk off.* **Ron** *and* **Yvonne** *sit in silence.* **Ron** *sips his can of beer.*

Ron   Mmmm.

Yvonne   What?

Ron   Interesting.

Yvonne   The man's a pig.

Ron   He's all right . . .

Yvonne   Try and get to know 'em?

Ron   It takes all sorts.

Yvonne   Oh he's just thick, Ron, admit it.

Ron   He's all right.

Yvonne   If he went to watch the sea lion show he probably wouldn't understand it! That's real life, that is. We're actually living on another planet, aren't we?

Ron   They're not in the fast lane, are they?

Yvonne   I don't think that they're in any lane to be brutally honest.

A beat.

Ron   She's all right though.

Yvonne   Meaning?

Ron   What?

Yvonne   Meaning?

Ron   Meaning, she's all right. She's great, full of it.

Yvonne   Oh leave it.

Ron   What?

Yvonne   That you feel sorry for her?

Ron   I never said a word.

Yvonne   You don't have to.

Ron   I have never said a word!

Yvonne   You can't save every disadvantaged kid in the world, Ron, that's what nearly killed you at school!

Ron   Some people just don't seem to stand a chance, do they?

Yvonne   Don't be so patronising.

Ron   I wasn't being, was I, I was being observant.

Yvonne   Well thankfully I'm not from your sort of background, so I don't have a problem with it. People either make something of their lives or they don't, and that's how it works. Don't make it your burden.

Ron   I'm not.

Yvonne   Good.

Ron   And anyway, don't tell me what to do.

Yvonne   What?

Ron   Don't tell me what to do.

Yvonne   I wasn't.

Ron   Yes you were.

Yvonne   Well I'm sorry.

Ron   Okay fine.

Yvonne   Go on then. Take on the burden of the dysfunctional if that's what rings your bell.

Ron   They're not dysfunctional. Now *you're* being patronising.

Yvonne   Well is there any wonder?

Ron   Well, you don't like it when I tell you what to do, do you? I mean, if I said: 'Don't go and see those strippers,' you wouldn't like it, would you?

Yvonne   Oh, so that's what this is about?

Ron   No!

Yvonne   I just wish you wouldn't be so . . .

Ron   What?

Yvonne   Anal!

Ron   Anal?

Yvonne   But you are!

Ron   Go on your run if you're going. I'll do all this. Even though it has an element of practicality about it. I'm sure I'll be able to do it. It'll be a challenge.

Yvonne   I can't believe you're being like this!

Ron   Like what?

Yvonne   You're repressed. That's your problem, always have been.

Ron   Where did all that come from, touched a sensitive nerve have I?

Yvonne   If you're going to make such a song and dance about it I won't go. I won't even go for a pizza, I'll stay here and change the chemical toilet or something!

Ron   Do you want to go?

Yvonne   No.

Ron   Oh come on!

Yvonne   You've never seen a stripper, have you?

Ron   Years ago. Sadly!

Yvonne   Funny!

Ron   Look, what can I say? I can't win. If I say I don't want you to go, I look repressive, if I say I want you to go, I look like I'm not bothered.

Yvonne   What are you scared of? Comparisons?

Ron   Spare me that. My hopes of being Mister Body Beautiful for the East Coast evaporated when I was twenty-one! I've seen myself in the mirror, and it's not pretty, you should know that.

Yvonne   Look, hundreds of women go, thousands.

Ron   I know and I'm not stopping you from going. But you don't seem to be hearing me!

Yvonne   I'm only going to see how the women behave.

Ron   So you are going now?

Yvonne   I'll not go.

Ron   But you want to go, don't you?

Silence.

Tell me the truth?

Yvonne   Yes.

Ron   Why?

Yvonne   Look, why are we arguing about this rubbish?

Ron   We're not arguing.

Yvonne   It's a bit of fun, that's all.

Ron   A bit of fun, oh right, is that all it is?

Yvonne   Oh Ron, it is.

Ron   Of course it is, how could it be anything else?

Yvonne   Come on . . . ?

Ron   When I started teaching I was on cover for a difficult fifth year group – as it was then known. I'd got them working and I was sat at the front writing up some notes for my M. Ed. as it happens. And these two lads got talking. One of them had been to a do at a golf club somewhere, Bradford I think. They'd had a comic on and then a stripper, and then another stripper. Then a bloke came around with the hat apparently, asking if they'd like to see an act, you know . . .

Yvonne   I've got the picture.

Ron   Well you can imagine what happened?

Yvonne   Yes I can, thank you!

Ron   Anyway according to this lad everybody ended up on stage, including him, fifteen he must have been. I don't know what really went on but by God the image has been imprinted on my brain for years. It was a brilliant laugh he said. A brilliant laugh. And do you know what, it just started as a bit of fun.

Yvonne   So what are you saying?

Ron   I'm saying it's a cruel world.

Yvonne   Oh the Oracle speaks!

Ron   Come out of your bubble.

Yvonne   I don't live in a bubble.

Ron   Book clubs, coffee mornings, amateur dramatics and decoupage? Early music? Yvonne, bloody hell, you live the life of Reilly. And now you want to go down into the swamp!

Yvonne   The swamp? Oh come on!

Ron   Well?

Yvonne   And you don't live the life of Reilly, do you? We've just bought that sodding thing for fourteen grand cash!

Ron   I see more of real life than you. Well I did.

Yvonne   Yes and look what it did to you?

Ron   You go if you want. I can't stop you going, can I?

Yvonne *stands to exit.*

Ron   Where are you going now?

Yvonne   For a run.

Ron At this time?

Yvonne Why not?

Ron So what shall I do with this spare food, put it in the fridge or bin it?

Yvonne *jogs off.* **Ron** *continues to put the rubbish into his plastic bag.*

Music.

Blackout.

Scene Thirteen.

Early the next evening.

Steph *enters, she is very dolled up with far too much flesh showing. She looks distinctly cheap.* **Ron** *comes from his caravan.*

Steph She ready?

Ron Just gone to the shower block. She says there isn't enough light in here. You look nice.

Steph It's just a bit of slap.

Ron No, looks great.

Steph I've plastered it on, I want to get down there. Do you know, I'm shaking already. Mind you, once we've got a few drinks down us we should be all right. Just think about us, down there watching all that flesh.

Ron I will do.

Steph Seems weird us down there and you up here reading a book or sommat!

Ron Well I've done my gallivanting.

Steph Oh aye?

Ron Oh aye, I've done my bit.

Steph   What and you a headmaster?

Ron   Never judge a book by its cover.

Steph   Why's that then?

Ron   It's a saying.

Steph   Oh you're full of 'em, aren't you?

Ron   What time does it start?

Steph   The main act's on at eight.

Ron   Oh right, I wonder if it'll have an interesting structure?

Yvonne *enters, looking much more attractive than before and up for the night ahead.*

Yvonne   You can't see a thing in there at this time of night, somebody's caked grass all over the mirror. Will this do, I mean I look like one of their mothers or something!

Steph   She looks great, doesn't she?

Yvonne   I don't.

Steph   Just think when she gets back, Ron, she'll want to ravish you!

Ron   What, more than she does now?

Steph   Come on, let's go and see all them muscles. I bet you can't wait, can you?

Yvonne   No that's right.

Steph   Don't wait up, hey if we get near the front we might never come back!

Ron   If you get near the front you might have an eye out.

Grant *enters, he is dressed for the night too.*

Grant   What've we got here then?

Steph   Arh you're only jealous because you're not coming.

Grant   Ah well I might come, that'd spoil it for you, wouldn't it?

Steph   He would come and all him just to spite us!

Grant   How do you know I'm not one of the strippers anyway?

Steph   Well if you are I want a chuffin' refund. What do you think?

Yvonne   Oh I don't know.

Grant   I've got everything they've got, you needn't worry about that!

Steph   Aye, but you've got some of it in the wrong place, love. You want to take some of that from round your middle and put it somewhere else.

Grant   Go on, you cheeky gett!

Steph   I bet he's going to follow us, aren't you?

Grant   You're joking, aren't you? Once those women down there catch sight of me them stripper efforts would stand no chance.

Steph   Oh yeh?

Grant   What do you reckon, Yvonne, do I look all right?

Yvonne   Better than he does.

She refers to **Ron**.

Ron   You two had better go if you're going. If you don't get there at the beginning you won't be able to follow the plot, will you?

Yvonne   I'll see you later then!

The women begin to move off.

I won't be late, ring the girls.

Ron   You just go and have a good time. And don't look!

Steph   That's the whole point, int it?

A beat.

Grant   She's been wanting to go for ages.

Ron   It's just a bit of fun, isn't it?

Grant   She says they go the whole way. I saw a documentary about it! They're just groups of lads who love the-sens, into t' body beautiful and all that. Arse-wipes I think, I wouldn't piss on 'em if they were burning in the street, half of 'em are queers anyway.

Ron   You reckon?

Grant   Half of 'em.

Ron   Really?

Grant   Queers.

Ron   No worries there then?

Grant *farts loudly.*

Grant   Get out and walk. Sea's calm, should be a nice night.

Ron   You reckon?

Grant   Tha can come down for a drink if tha wants?

Ron   No thanks. I'll just . . .

Grant   Please thee-sen.

Grant *is offended by his own stink.*

Good God that stinks! Sorry about that, better out than in!

Grant *walks off.* **Ron** *watches him go and then returns to his caravan and commences reading. As he does, Donna Summer's 'I Feel Love' plays under and swells.*

Scene Fourteen

The Futurist Theatre.

A corner of the stage is designated for the Futurist Theatre. **Steph** *and* **Yvonne** *are watching the strip show, as the Luigini fades, sexy pop music plays. As this happens the two women become completely engrossed in the show they are watching.* **Ron** *remains on stage for a while. Both* **Yvonne** *and* **Steph** *are drinking from bottles.*

Steph (*shouting*)   Get it off! Come on, get it off. (*To* **Yvonne**.) I like that one! The one with the tattoo!

Yvonne   Oh no!

Ron   What about the black one?

Yvonne   No.

Steph   Don't you like any of 'em?

Yvonne   The one with long hair.

Steph   Nice arse.

Yvonne   Well a big one anyway.

Steph   Nice big arse. Just one night with that and what you wouldn't do! Get your bloody teeth into that and you'd be laughing.

Yvonne   You might be, he wouldn't.

Steph   Bite his bloody arse off!

Both women laugh uproariously.

(*Shouts.*) Come on, big arse, show us what you've got!

Yvonne   Look at his stomach. Ron's was never like that.

Steph   Get your pants off, big arse. Get 'em off and throw 'em over here! Oh I like that one.

Yvonne   Which one?

Steph   The one with the chest.

Yvonne   They've all got bloody chests . . .

Steph   We'll have to get their autographs, won't we? Put some oil on it!

As the women narrate the event **Ron** *decides to get ready for bed.* **Ron** *goes into the caravan and puts his pyjamas on. Luigini swells slightly so there is a cacophony of noise.*

Come on, show us it then!

Yvonne   Come on!

Steph   Get 'em off.

Yvonne *to* **Steph**.

Yvonne   Do they take it all off?

Steph   They would if I had anything to do with it.

Yvonne   Oh he's nice this one!

Steph   Slow, slower. Oh, yes, that's it, that's it, nice and slow.

Throughout this **Ron** *is pulling on some styleless pyjamas, and he crawls into bed.*

Yvonne   Nice.

Steph   Firm. Oh God . . .

Yvonne   Turn around, turn around.

Steph   Full Monty, Full Monty . . .

Yvonne   Yes . . . ah, ah . . . Ah my God! Brilliant!

They both applaud.

Steph   Do you want another drink?

Yvonne   Well I shouldn't really.

Steph   Are you enjoying it?

Yvonne   No. It's absolutely awful!

Steph   Hey wait until it gets really going, they haven't even started yet!

Pop music swells.

Lights fade to black.

Scene Fifteen

Later that night.

The caravan site is quiet. **Ron** *is asleep.* **Grant** *stumbles back on to the site. He is quite drunk. He sings badly to himself. He has a couple of rabbits with him. He sits on the chairs outside* **Ron**'s *caravan. He switches on the cassette and JS Bach's 'Sheep May Safely Graze' plays.*

Grant   Not bad!

Grant *leaves a rabbit for* **Ron**. **Steph** *and* **Yvonne** *enter, drunk. A torch lights their way.*

Steph   Sssh.

Yvonne   Ron must be asleep.

Steph   You'll have to go and waken him.

Yvonne   Oh heck.

Grant   Back then?

Steph   Good night?

Grant   Mate of mine gave me some rabbits, there's one for you.

Yvonne   For me?

Grant   Have you ever had a bit of rabbit?

Yvonne   No.

Grant   It's nice is rabbit.

Yvonne   Oh thanks . . .

Grant   Skin it, and you'll be all right with that.

Yvonne   Skin it?

Grant   What was it like then?

Steph   Hey, this one here is off her head!

Yvonne   It's not me, it's you.

Steph   Got her up on stage.

Grant   Yeh?

Yvonne   I didn't know what was going on to be honest.

Steph   She was putting oil all over 'em!

Yvonne   Oh no, come on, he made me.

Steph   I think she could have been well in there.

Yvonne   I think I could.

Steph   They just grabbed her, didn't they?

Grant   Must have thought she needed it.

Yvonne   Bloody embarrassing, wasn't it?

Steph   No.

Yvonne   No?

Steph   Yes!

Yvonne   Yes!

Steph   You should've seen her face. I mean there's five hundred women there and they pick her.

Yvonne   I couldn't believe it!

Steph   Some were chucking their knickers!

Yvonne   I didn't want to get up but they got me, didn't they?

Steph   Two of 'em. One of them was that black one . . .

Yvonne God knows what I'm doing, then they spin me around about a dozen times. I didn't know what was going off. I'd already had four rum and cokes so I was dizzy before I got up there. Anyway so I'm oiling this other one, aren't I?

Steph You should've seen her!

Yvonne And I'm thinking, 'Hello, what are you doing?' And then this big one grabs me, didn't he . . .

Steph You should've seen her dancing . . .

Yvonne I'm just up there me, dancing with 'em. I couldn't get hold of them because they were that oily, it was like grabbing a bar of soap! Ooops, slipped out! Talk about laugh!

Yvonne *picks up a rabbit, looks at it, and momentarily swings it as a penis.*

Hey this is good.

Steph Oh nice.

Yvonne I don't like yours!

Steph Oh he's nice.

Yvonne Yeh?

Steph Nice arse.

Yvonne Oh yes!

Steph And you know what?

Yvonne What?

Steph He fucks like a rabbit!

Grant, **Yvonne** *and* **Steph** *fall about laughing.* **Ron** *(Malvolio-like) has emerged from the caravan half asleep. Stands watching.*

Yvonne *(noticing* **Ron**) Here he is, another one. Go on Ron, get 'em off. Show us what you've got and all. I'll do the music. Da, da, da, da . . . Come on! Show us your stomach muscles!

Yvonne *plays up to* **Ron**. *He stands.*

Ron   I thought you weren't drinking?

Yvonne   I've only had one.

Grant   One too many.

Ron   Come on, that's enough. Let's get you in bed.

Yvonne   Yes go on, go and get in that sleeping bag, so I can ravish you!

Steph   See, told you, didn't I? Told you your luck was in!

Ron   Yvonne?

Yvonne   All that nylon, wonderful! Hey, Ron, if they zip us up together there'd be that much friction, we'd set the bloody caravan on fire.

Ron   What can you do when they're drunk?

Yvonne *makes a drunken scene.*

Yvonne   There he is, look, the man who kept Doncaster Highfields School open, against all the odds; the man who gave everything to the education system and it sent him round the bend. Oh that's funny. You look really funny.

Ron   Come on, let's have you.

Yvonne   Let's have me? That'd be a turn up for the books!

Ron   Yvonne?

Yvonne   What a body?

Steph   Oooh . . .

Yvonne   Coooor! Just have a look at that, the sexiest man in the bloody world!

Ron   Yes very funny, very good!

All laugh, save **Ron**. **Yvonne** *flings the rabbit to* **Ron** *who catches it.* **Yvonne** *bursts into laughter as do* **Steph** *and* **Grant**. **Ron** *is not amused.*

Yvonne   Here, have a rabbit!

Music plays.

Lights fade.

Blackout.

End of Act One.

Act Two

Scene One

Early morning.

The lights come up on a very warm day. **Ron** *is sorting his gas bottle out, it ran out during the night and he is making sure it will not gas them.* **Steph** *comes out, she is looking very sexy in a short denim skirt, white clogs and a skimpy top. She smokes.*

Steph   Oh hell, the morning after, again!

Ron   Gas bottle!

Steph   Run out?

Ron   I forgot to turn the heating off. We were roasted during the night.

Steph   How is she?

Ron   Well she's suffering now I've had this on. She's down by the sea, a bottle of aspirin in one hand and a glass of liver salts in the other.

Steph   Not too well then?

Ron   She's felt better.

Steph   Well she was putting them away.

Ron   Oh she can do.

Steph   For every one I had she had two!

Ron   Well she's got three months' catching up to do, hasn't she? (*Blows his nose.*) Bloody hay fever.

Silence.

Steph   Grant's dead to the world. Mind you, he's like that most nights.

Ron   Thank him for the rabbit by the way. (*Sneezes.*) Ah the grass, it gets me in the mornings.

A beat.

Steph I'll tell you something, it was wild down there last night.

Ron Was it!

Steph But I think you've got to go crazy every now and again, don't you? Otherwise you'd go bloody mad!

Ron Maybe.

A beat.

Steph So do you?

Ron What?

Steph Go mad?

Ron Not any more.

Steph Oh boring!

Ron I just want to put my feet up and take it steady. And I've even gone the extra yard now I've bought that. It's a sure sign.

Ron *refers to the caravan.*

Steph Is it?

Ron You know when people buy cars they can be seen as penis extensions, can't they?

Steph Can they?

Ron Well you know, look at me I've got a big car?

Steph Have you?

Ron No, no, I haven't got a big car. I've got a family car.

Steph Well it looks like a big car.

Ron Yes, it is a big car, but that's not the point. It's not a penis extension.

Steph Isn't it?

Ron   No, it's just a big family car to pull the caravan. But the point is, now I've got a caravan, I've as much as said, 'Look at me I've opted out of the rat race, I've put my slippers under the awning.' Well actually I couldn't get the awning up, so if that's a metaphor for anything I'm snookered.

A beat.

Steph   How old are you then?

Ron   Me? Nearly forty-four.

Steph   Grant's that. And he's still got plenty of life left in him!

Ron   Yes but, what do they say: you're only as old as the woman you feel?

Steph   Who says that then?

Ron   It's a saying!

Steph   Oh that's good that is. Mind you, if it works the other way around it doesn't say a lot for me, does it?

Ron   No I don't suppose it does.

Steph   Anyway you're happy enough, aren't you?

Ron   Me?

Steph   You wouldn't want to trade Yvonne in for another model, would you?

Ron   Not with the same amount of mileage on anyway.

Steph   I bet she was wild when she was younger!

Ron   No not really. She was quite quiet when we met. It's that bloody long ago now I can't remember to be honest. No, most of the time she's reliable old Yvonne.

Steph   Well she knows how to enjoy herself.

Ron   Well she likes a laugh, you know, like the rest of us.

Steph   Not much. You've got a wild one there, I wouldn't let her out of my sight if I was you!

Ron   Well I don't think she'll get up to much this morning, not the way she was feeling at five o'clock.

Steph   I know, I still feel a bit rough.

Silence.

Ron   So it sounds like it was a good night?

Steph   It was a right scream.

Ron   Did they do the full bit then, you know, the full . . . bit?

Steph   What?

Ron   You know, all off?

Steph   Oh yeh!

Ron   Oh right.

Steph   Oh aye, it all comes off.

Ron   Oh right.

Steph   You can touch some of 'em if you're lucky enough. Mind you, what do you expect for seven quid?

Ron   Oh right.

Steph   Why, were you thinking of doing it?

Ron   Not me!

Steph   There were a lot of seven quids in there last night. Somebody's making a packet!

Ron   No, I'm too old for all that!

Steph   I've always liked older men to be honest.

Ron   Ah right!

Steph   No, I think older men are a lot more sorted.

Ron Do you?

Steph Don't you?

Ron Well I'm not.

Steph No I do.

Ron Anyway I don't think anyone would want to pay seven quid to see me get my kit off.

Steph Yvonne might.

Ron No.

Steph No?

Ron She's never liked parting with money at the best of times. I can't see her forking out seven quid for me to flash my bits.

Steph Not when she's seen most of 'em anyway!

Ron Most of 'em, how many do you think I've got?

Steph Well you never know.

Ron No, my stripping days are definitely over.

Steph Oh you see, boring.

Ron I showed my bum out of the back of a minibus once.

Steph Oh you devil!

Ron Must have been twenty years ago. I couldn't do it now, I'd probably get my arse stuck in the window or something.

A beat.

Steph Well I think you're sweet.

Ron Sweet?

Steph Yeh.

Ron That's about the least sexy thing you can ever say to a man.

Steph   What, even a boring one?

Ron   Anyway I'd better get this gas bottle sorted.

Steph   Oh don't take it personal. It was only a joke, I'm only pulling your leg. I mean, Yvonne's a wild woman, you'd have to have sommat special to be able to cope with her, wouldn't you?

Ron   Do you reckon?

Steph   Oh aye, you'd have to be some kind of bloody nutcase! Anyway I'll see you later. His lordship wants a bacon sarnie bringing. Sometimes it makes you wonder if it's all worthwhile, doesn't it?

Ron *stops and watches her go.*

Ron   Yes it does, doesn't it?

Music.

Blackout.

Scene Two

Later in the day.

A very weary **Yvonne** *comes back from her walk.* **Ron** *stands where we left him, though it is several hours later. He looks at her as she gently lowers herself into a chair.*

Ron   I thought you'd got lost!

Yvonne   Oh don't!

Ron   Still bad?

Yvonne   Not good!

Ron   The brain shrinks when you drink too much.

Yvonne   Well you drink everyday.

Ron   Yeh, my brain's about the size of a pea. I expect to lose it one day down a nostril.

Yvonne   Ohh, I feel rough.

Silence.

Ron   You won't fancy a bit of rabbit then? I've skinned it and cooked it, I thought you might try an eyeball or something?

Yvonne   Urghh!

Ron   The fur took some getting off but . . .

Yvonne   Ron . . . ?

Ron   I've had the back two legs myself. Tasty!

Yvonne   You haven't?

Ron   I'm joking.

Yvonne   What shall we do with it?

Ron   I've stuck it in the fridge.

Yvonne   Don't put it in the fridge! Bung it in the car boot!

Ron   He might want the skin back, or a foot or something. You're going to have to eat it!

Yvonne   Ron, I can't keep an aspirin down at the moment, so there is no way I'm going to eat a rabbit. Not now, not ever! I feel disgusted with myself as it is.

Ron   I told you not to go.

Yvonne   It's not the stripping, it's the drink.

Ron   So you had a good time then?

Yvonne   Actually it was quite well done, quite professional. If you must know!

Ron   Oh, come on?

Yvonne   It was.

Ron   Come on?

Yvonne   What?

Ron   No mention of dick size or bum quality?

Yvonne   What are you on about?

Ron   Just a modest, 'It was quite well done!' What are you hiding?

Yvonne   Nothing.

Ron   'It was quite well done?'

Yvonne   Oh don't!

Ron   'I liked the oiling down scene particularly, and I thoroughly enjoyed the bum massaging, but felt that the zip pulling ballet was thin on substance. Over all, quite well done.' Thank you, Yvonne Marlowe, theatre critic for the *Caravan Weekly*!

Yvonne   It was actually a good show!

Ron   Why don't you just tell me what it was really like?

Yvonne   Go yourself if you're so curious. I'll lend you a skirt!

Ron   'It was quite well done?'

Yvonne   It was professional.

Ron   You don't mean to tell me that's what you were thinking, while you were watching it?

Yvonne   I don't know what I was thinking.

Ron   I suppose when it finished one of them sang an aria for twenty minutes while the others danced about behind him?

Yvonne   It was actually quite stylish. Why do you mock everything I do?

A beat.

Ron   Well that's three months on the wagon, gone!

Yvonne   I mean, I had to have a drink to get through it!

Ron   Steph said you were putting them away.

Yvonne   It is very hard to be stone cold sober in that kind of atmosphere! Anyway you used to drink at the Amateurs. When we did *The Vagabond King* you were pissed most nights!

Ron   I've rung the girls by the way, everything's fine.

Yvonne   Did you tell them?

Ron   What, that you'd got drunk, and seen The Flying Dicks?

Yvonne   You're not going to let this drop, are you?

Ron   Grant the Grunt reckons they're all gay, but . . .

Yvonne   What did you say?

Ron   What could I say? 'Your mother's gone native, all this marathon running and health food is just a front, deep down she's really a raving voyeur'?

Yvonne   Why do I bother?

Ron   I told them you'd gone for a jog. Why, you're not ashamed of yourself, are you?

Yvonne   Well I shouldn't be, but you make me feel like I am.

A beat.

Well say something.

Ron   Don't you worry about it. You're a well-educated, sensitive, attractive, highly sexual, married mother of three, who's stuck with a neurotic, old fart.

Yvonne   You said that!

Ron   It's absolutely natural that you should want to go and watch six handsome young blokes parade their manhood, I mean who wouldn't?

Yvonne   Sometimes!

Ron   It's the animal button, isn't it? It's either on or off. And yours is obviously on. I suppose some people can never turn theirs off!

Yvonne   You can.

Ron   Well I'm the exception, aren't I? I mean we can't all be perfect.

Love-making noises can be heard coming from the caravan nearby.

Steph   Oh, oh, oh, oh, oh.

Ron   Here we go! Just in time for the matinee.

Steph   Oh, oh, oh!

Ron   Early today, aren't they?

Yvonne   It's too hot in there surely?

Ron   You've got to admire their durability, haven't you? Three o'clock in the afternoon and the chocks are off! Everybody else is relaxing but not the Grunts!

Steph   Oh, oh.

Ron   I might eat that rabbit myself when I think about it. It certainly works for him!

Yvonne   Oh hell.

Ron   This is just . . . Isn't it bizarre, utterly ridiculous! Why does he have to do that? Does he think we can't hear?

Yvonne   It's not him, is it, it's her.

Ron   What do you mean?

Yvonne   Well she's making all the fuss.

Ron   But he starts it off.

Yvonne What's wrong, are you jealous?

Ron I probably am, now you come to mention it!

Yvonne You are, aren't you?

Ron I'd never last the course, would I? Not with somebody like Steph. Be honest. I'd probably twist my back and come out bent double. I mean, they must have detachable limbs or something. Because if I even try and make a cup of tea in ours, I tie myself in knots!

Steph Oh, oh . . .

Ron I can't sit here listening to this. I thought we might go out on a boat. They've refurbished the *Hispaniola*.

Yvonne Not a chance.

Ron It goes across the bay . . .

Yvonne I think I'm going to need some stronger tablets. Do we have any Nurofen?

As **Yvonne** *gets up to go into the caravan the noise from* **Steph** *changes tone.*

Steph No Grant, no, please no, Grant! Grant no . . .

Ron Oh right!

Steph No no no . . . oh oh . . .

Yvonne Is she all right?

Ron How do I know?

Steph No, please . . .

Yvonne That sounds a bit . . .

A beat.

Why don't you go and find out?

Ron Find out what?

Yvonne What's going on.

Steph   No, no Grant please . . .

Ron   What am I going to do?

Yvonne   Well it sounds a bit . . .

Ron   I know it sounds a bit . . .

Steph   Please no . . . oh, oh!

Yvonne   Ron, do something.

Ron   What?

Yvonne   I don't know!

Ron   What if it's all part of it?

Yvonne   All part of what?

Ron   The thing?

Yvonne   What thing?

Ron   The animal thing?

Yvonne   What are you on about?

Ron   Oh, come on . . . !

Yvonne   Ron, I've got a splitting head, I'm dying here, don't play twenty questions with me!

Ron   What if it's a game?

Yvonne   It doesn't sound like a game.

Ron   But what if it is one?

Yvonne   It sounds too real.

Ron   What if they're playing, 'Slap me, slap me'?

Yvonne   Eh?

Ron   Slap me, slap me!

Yvonne   What sort of bloody game is that?

Ron   Oh, come on!

Yvonne   Slap me, slap me?

Ron   I say 'No', but I mean 'Yes'.

Steph   Oh, oh, no . . .

Ron   I mean, what if I suddenly storm in there and discover they're sat reading the papers and smoking.

Steph   No, no. Grant no please, no. Oh.

Yvonne   I think you should do something!

Ron   You do something.

Yvonne   Like what?

Ron   Throw some water over them or something. That's what my dad used to do with the dog.

Yvonne   Oh God I feel awful.

Ron   I suppose we could go.

Yvonne   Eh?

Ron   We could just go.

Yvonne   Why?

Steph   Oh, oh, oh!

Ron   That's why? That's what's great about having a caravan, you go to one place, and if you don't like it, you go somewhere else.

Yvonne   We can't go, it looks bad.

Ron   And this doesn't look bad, living next door to Fred and Wilma Flintstone?

Yvonne   I thought they were all right? I thought you could cope with them because you were from the same background, what happened to all that?

Ron *walks across the pitch. And shouts.*

Ron   Hello?

Yvonne   Ron?

Ron   Hello! We can hear you? We know what you're doing?

Steph   Oh, oh, oh! No . . .

Ron shouts.

Ron   Shut up for God's sake, give it a bloody rest!

Yvonne   Ron, stop shouting please!

Ron   I can't believe this.

Yvonne   I can't go anywhere, I feel so awful!

Steph   Oh, oh! Oh . . .

The noise stops.

Yvonne   They've stopped.

Ron   Only to re-fuel.

Yvonne   Oh my bloody head!

Ron   I never saw it like this. I'd got it down as seagulls squawking and the smell of cow shit.

Yvonne   The man's a pig.

Ron   I don't know about you, but my imagination is working overtime.

Yvonne   Do you think we should do something?

Ron   Like what?

Yvonne   Well, report them.

Ron   Who to?

Yvonne   Well the site warden or somebody, call the police. Just as a precaution.

Ron   Report them, what for?

Yvonne   Well . . . ?

Ron Yes, 'Hello, is that the police, well we've heard some aggressive love-making going on in the next caravan, and we don't think it's normal.' 'Well what were you doing listening, sir? Haven't you got anything better to do?'

Yvonne I mean, you never know, do you?

Ron Well, no, you don't, but . . .

Yvonne He treats her like she's one of his bloody dogs or something. I've a good mind to say something to him.

Ron Don't say a word for God's sake.

Yvonne If you ever did that sort of thing to me I'd leave you.

Ron What sort of thing?

Yvonne Well whatever's making her shout like that!

Ron If I ever did that sort of thing to you, love, I'd need a back up team!

Yvonne *walks towards the other caravan.*

Yvonne Don't be bloody funny!

Ron Where are you going? Come away. Leave it be!

Yvonne I think she puts some of that on, you know? She must know we can hear!

Ron So who's she putting it on for?

Yvonne Well it's not me.

Ron Well it's not for me, is it?

Yvonne I don't know.

Ron It's obviously for the Grunt isn't it?

Yvonne Oh listen, I think they're starting again?

Ron Oh I'm going, I can't stand another bout of that.

Ron *is about to lift the gas bottle.*

Yvonne   Where are you going?

Ron   I'm going to refill the gas bottle.

Yvonne   Ron, it's absolutely boiling, we don't need the heating on.

Ron   No, but after all that thrashing about I need a strong cup of tea. Besides this looks like the only exercise I'll be getting this holiday!

Music.

Blackout.

Scene Three

Later that afternoon.

Grant *comes out of the caravan. He has a large bowl of potato peelings. As he walks out* **Steph** *comes to him with some empty cans of beans, and a carrier bag.*

Steph   Here, take the rest of the rabbit giblets!

Grant   Leave that foot that I've left on the sink, I want to make our Josh a keyring.

Steph   You've forgotten half the bloody rubbish. Why are you so useless?

Grant   Thought you'd finished!

Steph   And look at me eye, I'm going to have a right shiner there.

Grant   It'll be all right.

Steph   It will, I'll look a right fuckin' mess.

Grant   It wa' an accident.

A beat.

Steph   Are they about?

Grant   He's gone for a walk, don't know where she is.

Steph   Ron says she felt like shit.

Grant   Oh dear!

Steph   I was thinking. They've got some nice stuff, haven't they?

Grant   Aye, we'll have some of that.

Steph *looks at* **Ron/Yvonne**'s *chairs.*

Steph   Nice chairs, mind you they're mucky to say they're new.

Grant   And I tell you sommat else.

Steph   What?

Grant   She's got mucky knickers.

Steph   You what?

Grant   Her knickers are filthy. I'd chuck most of 'em out if I was her.

Steph   Since when have you seen her knickers?

Grant   She wants to get some new uns. Typical of that type, they come all the new caravan and their knickers are hung on the line, falling to bloody bits. I wouldn't let you wear what she wears.

Steph   She's all right!

Grant   I'm not saying she int. She likes a drink and a laugh, and that's fair enough. But I don't think she has much fun wi' him, does she?

Grant *is inspecting* **Ron**'s *caravan. He looks at the lock on the hitch.*

Nice caravan though.

Steph   He's all right.

Grant   He's a fart.

Steph   Oh God, sometimes!

Grant   Look at that, they've got the top of the range lock on it and all. Bloody hell. See! They must have some money! Top of the range lock. Sixteen quid that. You can get one for four pound. I mean, why put a top of the range lock on? It's all for bloody show!

Steph   They're all right, a bit starchy but . . . she's a laugh really!

Grant *looks at the caravan on stage.*

Grant   Fourteen grand?

Steph   Nice.

Grant   Never worth that.

Steph   Nice though.

Grant   You lose three grand the minute you put it on a site.

Steph   You lose another three when we pull up.

Grant   You bloody do and all! Mind you, that's a good van. I know it's had some stick, but it's as good a van as there is on this site!

Steph   I could live with that no trouble.

Grant   Needs an awning on it to finish it off though.

Steph   She told me he's useless, couldn't put it up.

Grant   Bloody easy.

Steph   Couldn't do it though, not without the instructions. She said he has to have the instructions for everything or he's hopeless.

Grant   I thought he was a bloody headmaster? Thought he was supposed to be bloody genius or sommat?

Steph   Do you want any peas with this or what?

Grant *is looking in the van.*

Grant   Yeh, I'll have some peas. Hey they've got all fancy stuff in here, look!

Steph   Are you going to take that rubbish?

Grant   Ar.

Steph *starts to go back to her caravan. As she does* **Grant** *has a look around* **Ron**'s *caravan. And then sees their waste bin and puts his rubbish in their waste bin.*

Steph   Don't do that, you ignorant gett!

Grant   Fuck 'em!

Grant *bursts into laughter.* **Steph** *looks at him and laughs as well.*

Steph   You bloody idiot!

Music plays.

Blackout.

Scene Four

Later.

Grant *is sat relaxing in one of his chairs, he has a can of beer.* **Yvonne** *enters after having just been for a jog. She is sweating heavily.*

Yvonne   Oh! I sometimes wonder if it's all worthwhile.

Grant   Looks like horse work!

Yvonne   I thought it might clear my head.

Grant   This clears mine.

He refers to the beer bottle.

Yvonne   I think I feel worse.

Grant   It's too warm, isn't it?

Yvonne   It is now, I'm boiling.

Yvonne *peels off her jogging top. She has been sweating.* **Grant** *looks at her. We see the shape of her torso. Patches of sweat.*

Grant   Aye, it's warm today.

Yvonne   It is after six miles.

Grant   Worked up a sweat then?

Yvonne   Yes, I needed to.

Grant   Aye, looks like you've worked up a sweat. I like a good sweat.

Yvonne   You'll not sweat much doing that.

Grant   Oh I dunno. Anyway I've done my sweating for today.

Yvonne *reclines and gets her breath back.*

Yvonne (*breathless*)   Really?

Grant   I like feeling it run down my face.

Yvonne (*tired*)   Oh dear!

Grant   She says you're running the marathon?

Yvonne   Hoping to.

Grant   Must be fit then?

Yvonne   What?

Grant   Must be fit for that?

Yvonne   I don't feel it today.

Grant   I don't fancy it myself.

Yvonne   Well . . .

Grant   I reckon it's boring.

Yvonne   It is. You have to go through things in your head. It helps me work things out.

Grant   I've seen it on the telly but . . .

Yvonne   I watched it last year and wanted to do something different.

A beat.

Grant   Like doing things that are different, do you?

Yvonne   Well . . .

Grant   You like doing different things then?

Yvonne   Within reason.

Grant   Makes a change I bet.

Yvonne   I think I'd draw the line at parachuting. I don't think Ron would like it much anyway.

Grant   Keeps you on a short lead, does he?

Yvonne   Sorry?

Grant   I say, he likes to keep his eye on you?

Yvonne   Well?

Grant   See what you're up to?

Yvonne   Not really.

Grant   So he's not bothered what you do then?

Yvonne   Well . . .

Grant   I think you've got to keep an eye on 'em all the time. I have her. She's a right bloody headcase.

Yvonne   She is, she led me astray.

Grant   Oh!

Yvonne   Yes I'm afraid.

Grant   Oh!

Yvonne   What?

Grant   That's not what she said.

Yvonne   No?

Grant   Oh no.

Yvonne   Well there you go.

A beat.

Grant   Mind you, I've got dogs like that, you know?

Yvonne   Like what?

Grant   That you can't let loose?

Yvonne   Yes I bet you have!

Grant   You've got to keep a fuckin' chain on 'em or they'd be off sniffin' around any old bitch.

Yvonne   I'm sure.

A beat.

Grant   You had your rabbit yet?

Yvonne   Not yet.

Grant   You want to get it eaten before it turns. Has he ever skinned one before?

Yvonne   I wouldn't have thought so.

Grant   I'll come and do it for you if you want? If he doesn't know how to do it!

Yvonne   Well let's see how he gets on!

A beat.

Grant   Steph said it was a good night?

Yvonne   Oh that?

Grant (*laughs*)   Ah?

Yvonne   What?

Grant   Bloody women!

Yvonne   What about us?

Grant   You're all the same.

Yvonne   You think so?

Grant   Argh dear!

Yvonne   What?

Grant   I mean, I'm not against it. We've had it our way for long enough, haven't we?

Yvonne   Yes, I think you have.

Grant   Mind you, she said you went for it!

Yvonne   Anyway . . . !

Grant   Trying to forget about it, eh?

Yvonne   Trying to.

Grant   It's only human nature int it, it's like I told her . . . Nowt to be ashamed on.

Yvonne   I'd better get a shower and . . .

Yvonne *moves towards her caravan.*

Grant   Aye, she said that they were baying for blood down there last night. Mind you, I says, that's what it's for, int it, them as not getting any.

Yvonne   It was a good night actually!

Grant   I says, she'll not want to go and see them strippers but when she gets there she'll probably go bloody loopy!

Yvonne   Well . . . ?

Grant   It happens wi't dogs. You chain 'em up for that long, when you let 'em off they'd bloody kill you if they got you.

Yvonne   Right.

Grant   They'd never get me though, I'm too quick for 'em!

Yvonne   It was a good night. The pizza was a bit of a let-down but we had quite a laugh.

Grant   Aye, but she said that you were well out of order!

Yvonne   She said that, did she?

Grant   I said, bloody typical.

Yvonne   Actually . . .

Grant   Oh aye, trying to get out of it now, are you?

Yvonne   Wait till I see her.

Grant *stands with his drink. Finishes it off.*

Grant   Anyway, I'd better get some ale in. You don't want owt bringing do you? Or has he put the mockers on you having any more?

Yvonne   I don't feel like any at the moment.

Grant   You should see her in there, she can sup more than me, and that's saying something.

Yvonne   Now, I don't believe that for one minute.

Grant   It's right!

Yvonne   I think I've had enough to last me a whole year.

Grant   Arh can't trust yourself, eh?

Yvonne   I don't like being out of control . . .

Grant   Just like her in there, when she's had a few drinks she's absolutely anybody's.

Yvonne   Well I wouldn't go that far!

Grant   I've got to watch her like a fuckin' hawk sometimes!

Grant *exits.* **Yvonne** *watches as he goes.*

Music plays.

Blackout.

Scene Five

Later, evening.

Yvonne *is in the caravan. We find* **Ron** *facing* **Yvonne** *as the lights come up. It is quite dim inside. He is making some sandwiches.*

Ron   Well what do you expect from him, Shakespeare's sonnets?

Yvonne   He's so . . .

Ron   What?

Yvonne   Brutal!

Ron   The man breeds bull terriers, you're not going to get any coffee morning banter from him, are you?

Yvonne   He's got the social skills of a slug, honestly!

Ron   Well dogs don't talk a lot unless you hadn't noticed.

Yvonne   It's the way he looks at you and grunts.

Ron   Ham or cheese?

Yvonne   Ham.

Ron *continues making tea.*

Ron   There was a lad at school like him, he used to scare me to bloody death.

Yvonne   He sits there with his belly, urgh dear!

Ron   He made my life a misery. Danny Ward. Big Danny Ward. God he was rough. Rough as a bear's arse. I think he was shaving when he was ten. Every day he took my dinner tickets, every day for five years. I never thought of it as bullying at the time, but I suppose it was really. God knows what he did with them, he must have had thousands of my bloody dinner tickets!

Yvonne   He keeps going on about last night. He's so bloody thick, obviously can't cope with it, and he's got nothing else to talk about.

Ron   He's all right really.

Yvonne   God knows what she told him. It's the way he looks at you; (*as* **Grant**) 'Seen them strippers, ooh.' He's like a cartoon.

Ron   The country's full of men like him, Yvonne, they're called people. You need to get out more!

Yvonne   And they always seem to be attracted to me. And what she's doing with him, I just don't know! I mean she's really naive, and sweet and . . .

Ron   She's great, I told you.

Ron *hands a sandwich to* **Yvonne**.

Yvonne   What does she see in him even?

Ron   Well he's obviously good at one thing, isn't he? And I don't think they teach that at school.

Yvonne   No, if they had done I suspect you would have studied it to degree level.

Ron   Well 'A' level at least!

Yvonne   She was telling me about what they get up to.

Ron   Oh right.

Yvonne   Very frank and open.

Ron   Don't tell me it'll only depress me.

Yvonne   How could she possibly sleep with him. He's such a pig. And he's done that twice now!

Ron   Done what?

Yvonne   Been hanging about.

Ron   Well what do you want him to do? We're almost sleeping together, aren't we? Is he out there by the way?

Ron *looks out of the window.*

Yvonne   No he's gone to swing on the tyres I think.

Ron   Oh we shouldn't mock him really.

Yvonne   It's just how he is always floating about.

Ron   Well we're sharing a pitch, kid. What do you want me to say, 'Stop talking to my wife, she's reading all sorts into it.'

Yvonne   You don't have to read into it.

Ron   That's what passes for badinage, that's the banter of the workplace! Didn't you do Bernstein's language codes at Oxford?

Yvonne   Not on the music course.

Ron   Welcome to the real world.

A beat. With a mouthful of bread.

Yvonne   So you don't think we should do anything about it?

Ron   Anything about what?

Yvonne   About all that noise.

Ron   There's nothing that needs doing, is there?

Yvonne   Well no, except for the fact that there is a man across the way who is knocking a woman about . . .

Ron   We don't know that!

Yvonne   Well he's using insinuating behaviour . . .

Ron   Yvonne, lighten up, we're on a caravan site.

A beat.

Yvonne   Well, I think that we should go.

Ron   Are you serious?

Yvonne   Yes I am. We've had a trial, haven't we? I mean, we've worked out how everything works?

Ron   Yes, but . . . ?

Yvonne   I'd like to get home to be honest.

Ron   Why, do you still feel hungover?

Yvonne   Well I don't feel brilliant.

Ron   Oh great, you make a fool of yourself and we've got to go home!

Yvonne   Well I can't say I'm enjoying it, can you?

Ron   Yes, it's fine!

Yvonne   Well I'm not.

Ron   You were loving it before Steph and Grant pulled up!

Yvonne   It was all right.

Ron   Well we might as well sell the soddin' thing then.

Yvonne   Why are you always so extreme?

Ron   Fourteen grand down the bloody pan. What do you think we'll get for it? We'd be lucky to get ten. Ten grand and we've slept in it once.

Yvonne   I didn't say we should sell it. I just think we should be more choosey with the sites.

Ron   It was last minute, you know it was. All the Caravan Club sites were booked up.

Yvonne   Well we should try one of them, I mean this is just a field, isn't it?

Ron   They are all just fields!

Yvonne   Yes but . . .

Ron   I mean, I can't help it if you feel humiliated about last night.

Yvonne   I don't feel humiliated.

A beat.

Ron   Well I suppose we'll just have to go in the morning then. Jeez . . . !

Yvonne   We can see if there's any vacancies on the way back.

Ron   It'll probably take me four days to pack the bloody car up again. I'm just going to load everything in the van and that's it. I'm not listing everything, it's a waste of time. Meanwhile, don't go hanging your knickers on the clothesline.

Yvonne   What are you saying, that I'm leading him on?

Ron   No!

Yvonne   Yes!

Ron   No!

Yvonne   That's what you're saying.

Ron   I'm not saying that.

Yvonne   Yes you are.

Ron   Well it might have helped if you hadn't given him the full story and started swinging the rabbit about? You could see he was getting off on it!

Yvonne   You come out with such rubbish at times for an educated man.

Ron   And you do some bloody silly things for an educated woman.

Yvonne   You never support me, do you?

Ron   I'm not getting into it. You want to go tomorrow, we'll go tomorrow, I don't want to get into the rights and wrongs of what's gone off, I want to forget it.

Yvonne   You never do, you never do anything to support me.

Ron   What do you want me to do, go and give the Grunt a good hiding?

Yvonne   You've never done that yet.

Ron   You want the bloody good hiding if anybody.

Yvonne   Oh grow up, little boy!

Ron   I'm a little boy? You've been caught playing naughty and you want to go home. Ah dear me!

Yvonne   You don't know what it's like having somebody look at you all the time! He just looks at me, I could slap him I could!

Ron   Yes we're both agreed, the man's a bloody animal for God's sake. So why don't you go over and wallop him, you're the one doing all the training?

Yvonne   I might.

Ron   Oh very good.

Yvonne   I might do yet.

Ron   In fact, why don't you go over and ask him for a session because that's what you're really after!

Silence.

Yvonne   What?

Ron   That's what it all seems like to me!

Yvonne   Oh you are just pathetic sometimes, do you know that?

Yvonne *storms out of the caravan and exits.*

Ron   Yes love, you tell me every day!

Music.

Blackout.

Scene Six

An hour later.

Steph *comes from her caravan with some food remnants. She now has a decent black eye.* **Ron** *is packing up the awning as she comes out.*

Steph   Hiya!

Ron   Oh hiya! Just sorting this out. Lost without the instructions.

Steph   She feeling any better?

Ron   Yes, I think so, she's had a jog, sweated some of it out.

Steph   Yeh, Grant said he'd had a nice little chat!

Ron   Have you taken a bang?

Steph   Eh?

Ron   Your eye . . . ?

Steph   Accident.

Ron   Right.

Steph   You know what it's like, can't swing a cat . . .

Ron   I wondered because we heard some shouting earlier but . . .

Steph   Sorry about that.

Ron   No problem as long as everything's okay.

Steph   Did you hear?

Ron   I think they heard you in Newcastle to be honest.

Steph   Shit!

Ron   In fact, I think they could pick some of it up in Holland.

Steph   Have I gone red?

Ron   No but I did.

Steph   It's Grant he's bloody crackers . . .

Ron   Is he about?

Steph   He's gone to the site next door. It's talent night so he's trying to get me booked in. I'm doing Cher, 'Gypsies, Tramps and Thieves'.

Ron   Oh right. Great!

Steph   We're not supposed to go into the club but Grant knows somebody. I won thirty quid one weekend.

Ron   Really?

Steph   Yeh, I know, not bad is it?

As they chat **Grant** *comes on to the pitch. He has a large cardboard crate of beer with him.*

Grant   Come on, woman, put the bloody kettle on! Don't just stand there!

Steph   Listen to him . . . Who does he think he is?

Grant   Look at this, twenty-five quid for this lot. Ronnie said they'd fallen off the back of a warehouse.

Steph   Have you booked me on?

Grant   Quarter to nine. You're on after some twat doing Buddy Holly. And some kids doing Boyzone!

Steph   Oh there's always Buddy Holly.

Steph *goes inside the caravan.*

Grant   She's doing Cher.

Ron   She said.

Grant   'Gypsies, Tramps and Thieves'. I mean, it's thirty quid a pop, not bad you know, nearly pay for a week up here.

Ron   That's right.

Grant   I like it when she does Kate Bush the best . . . 'Oh me I'm Cathy, I'm coming home.' Whatever the fuck it is.

Ron   Sounds good!

Grant   You ought to get Yvonne across, if she's a bit of a singer.

Ron   Yes, that's right.

Grant   See how good she is. Who could she do?

Ron   No idea.

Grant   She couldn't do Cilla Black, could she?

Ron   No, I don't think she's right for that.

Grant   And she's not Tina Turner, is she?

Ron   No. Lesley Garratt?

Grant   Lulu.

Ron   Lulu?

Grant   I tell you what . . .

Ron   Go on . . .

Grant   Dusty Springfield!

Ron   You reckon?

Grant   Oh aye, she's a spit!

Ron   Yes, now you come to mention it . . .

Grant   Easy, she's easily Dusty Springfield int she, or Bonnie Tyler? She might even get away with Blondie!

Ron   Yeh?

Grant (*sings badly*)   'I just don't know what to do with myself!'

Ron   That's right.

Grant   Good song that . . .

Ron (*sings badly*)   'I'm so used to doing, everything with you . . .'

Grant   'I just don't know what to do . . .' That's right.

Ron   That's right.

Grant (*sings*)   'I just don't know what to do with my time!'

Both men join in a fairly poor few lines of the song.

Ron   I don't think we should enter.

Grant   Oh us, no chance, but she's easily Dusty Springfield int she? I mean, she's got the gob ant she?

Ron   That's right.

A beat.

Grant   I can't handle the bloody heat to be honest. Are you having one?

Grant *tears a beer from the crate.*

Ron   Not for me.

Grant   Mention it to her, then we can come back and have a few! Get a barbie going maybe . . .

Ron   That'd be good . . .

Grant   I can get some more rabbits if you want?

Ron   Well I think we can manage at the moment, thanks.

Grant   It's funny her doing singing and all int it?

Ron   Eh?

Grant   Yvonne and Steph, both of 'em are into singing?

Ron   Oh yes!

Grant   But Yvonne's funny int she when she's had a few. When she was playing with that rabbit! Funny!

Ron   It was, wasn't it?

Grant   I'd like to see her up there. I'd like to see if she can put it over, you know, because she's got it all, hasn't she, all the attitude?

Ron   That's right . . .

Grant   Well I'd better help her get ready or I'll be getting a black eye.

Grant *picks up his crate and makes to exit. Suddenly spins and stops.*

Tell her I'll give her a knock. Dusty Springfield, you tell her!

Ron   I will.

Grant   Hey, I've just had a thought.

Ron   What?

Grant   You never know, she might even get away with Petula Clarke!

Grant *exits.* **Ron** *goes back to the awning.*

Music.

Blackout.

Scene Seven

Half an hour later.

Ron *and* **Yvonne** *are outside their caravan.* **Ron** *is laughing and animated.* **Yvonne** *is preparing to tidy away their garden furniture.*

Ron   Oh be fair!

Yvonne (*moderately loud*)   I'm not going!

Ron   Keep your voice down.

Yvonne   Just go and tell him we're busy.

Ron   You tell him!

Yvonne   What's wrong, are you scared?

Ron   He's invited us out.

Yvonne   To a talent night on the site next door? It's my complete *bête noir*!

Ron   We've got to go.

Yvonne   You go if you're so keen.

Ron   Oh we've got to go.

Yvonne   I can't bear things like that, they're so tacky.

Ron   You went to that one on the cruise, you enjoyed that!

Yvonne   It was on the *Orianna* for goodness sake!

Ron   Well you tell the Grunt that!

Yvonne   Oh no, Ron, I can't go, no way. Anyway we've got to pack. Tell him that. Tell him I'm not so well.

Ron   You'll have to go because your mate's giving her Cher.

Yvonne   What?

Ron   Steph's doing Cher.

Yvonne   Oh my God!

Ron   Early stuff . . .

Yvonne   Oh hell . . . I can just imagine it.

Ron   'Gypsies, Tramps and Thieves'.

Yvonne   Oh no, I can't bear it! I bet it's awful.

Ron   And then he wants us to come back and have a barbecue . . .

Yvonne   No Ron, no!

Ron   He's bought a crate.

Yvonne   No!

Ron   It gets better.

Yvonne   It can't possibly get any worse, that's for sure.

Ron   He wants you to enter the talent contest.

Yvonne   No!

Ron   That's what he says.

Yvonne   No!

Ron   He's going to come and give you a knock.

Yvonne   No!

Ron   Oh you can't do this, this is what caravanning is all about.

Yvonne   I am not singing.

Ron   You've got to. He thinks you're having a good time.

Yvonne   How wrong he is!

Ron   Obviously it was the rabbit swinging that impressed him!

Yvonne   There is no way I am going, now you can tell him or I will.

A beat.

Ron   Well he reckons you could do a good Dusty Springfield.

Yvonne   Don't be bloody ridiculous!

Ron   I'm not being, he thinks you'd get away with Dusty Springfield.

Yvonne   Dusty Springfield?

Ron   Or Blondie at a push!

Yvonne   One of you is mad!

Ron   We've just been stood here singing the bloody lyrics.

Yvonne   I'm not doing it! Forget Dusty Springfield.

Ron *laughs.*

Ron   All right, all right. What about Petula Clarke then?

Yvonne   You're serious, aren't you?

Ron *tries to cajole* **Yvonne**.

Ron   Oh laugh!

Yvonne   Why?

Ron   Laugh at it.

Yvonne   I can't!

Ron   Laugh at it, Yvonne.

Yvonne   Why, it's not funny. It's bloody tragic. It's a nightmare.

Ron   It bloody is.

Yvonne   I am not singing in a talent competition on a caravan site no way, never ever! I'd rather die. I'd rather run through the streets naked. I'd rather be hung, drawn and quartered. No, no, no!

Silence.

Ron   Oh go on, I'll buy you a drink!

Ron *laughs uproariously.* **Yvonne** *has to smile.*

Music.

Blackout.

Scene Eight

Three hours later.

Ron *and* **Yvonne** *remain on stage, they are given drinks.* **Steph**, *who is dressed in a short black skirt with a moderate attempt at Cher, smokes and looks at the coast. A large number of crisps, hot dogs, empty cans of cheap beer and sandwiches are on stage. The barbecue has just come to an end. Its embers still glow.* **Grant** *enters with some more cans of beer. Everyone has had a bit too much to drink already. He offers one to* **Yvonne**.

Grant   Here you are, Yvonne, have another, there's plenty more where that came from! I know you like a drink, lass!

Yvonne   This is my last.

Grant   Famous last words! You'll not be running many marathons on that.

Yvonne   Not tonight anyway!

Grant   There's some more pork chops if anybody's interested. She always buys too much, don't you, cock?

Steph   Do I?

Grant   Nice burgers! I got 'em off a bloke at the club, he buys 'em for the site. The thing about barbecues is, if you cook it too long, you burn it, and if you undercook it, everybody gets the shits, don't you reckon, Yvonne?

Yvonne   That's right!

Ron   I thought you did a good job. I try but I make a real mess of it. That's another thing I'm not very good at.

Yvonne   Ron's okay if you like your food very, very burnt!

Grant   You all right, Steph?

Steph   Yeh!

A beat.

Grant   Well I was impressed, weren't you, Steph?

Steph   Yeh!

Grant   Yes, I was impressed. Very good, Yvonne? Don't you think, cock?

Steph   Not bad!

Grant   She's got the fuckin' mood on because she didn't win.

Steph   I haven't!

Grant   She can't win every time, can she, Ron?

Ron   No, but I thought she was terrific.

Steph   I wasn't!

Grant   Steph, Yvonne's studied singing hasn't she, you slack gett! She's bound to be bloody good.

Yvonne   I don't think studying it . . .

Grant   Shut up a minute you, she's got to be told . . . She's like this every time sommat doesn't go her way. If you're not pleasing her she's a bloody pain.

Ron   I thought Steph did well . . .

Grant   She did, I'm not saying she didn't, only you can tell class, can't you?

Ron   Well Yvonne's done a lot you see . . .

Grant   Mind you, you let me down, Yvonne. I wish you'd have done Dusty Springfield.

Yvonne   It's not my . . .

Grant   Shirley Bassey's all right though. (*Sings.*) 'Goldfinger!' Do it again.

Yvonne   No I . . .

Grant (*sings*)   'Goldfinger, he's the man, the man with the Midas touch . . .'

Yvonne Very good!

Ron Excellent!

Grant (*sings*) 'Goldfingaaar!'

Yvonne You've got it.

Grant Hey Steph, what do you think, 'Goldfingaaar'. Do you think I'd win?

Steph No.

Yvonne You've got the mouth for it anyway.

Grant Now I have got a gob on me! Hey, at least you didn't do any of that classical stuff. I thought when you got up there. I thought for God's sake don't do any classical stuff, some of them in that club are right bloody philistines.

Yvonne That's what I thought.

Ron I thought it was quite pleasant.

Grant Bloody heathens some of them. Pigs!

Steph Grant!

A beat.

Grant So, go on then, what did you think of the talent?

Yvonne Well . . .

Grant Go on . . .

Yvonne Pretty average.

Ron Yvonne?

Yvonne Pretty average really.

Grant Really?

Yvonne In fact, I thought some of it was dreadful, to be honest.

Steph Oh right!

Yvonne   Well Buddy Holly looked more like John Major for a start.

Ron   Yvonne!

Yvonne   Well he couldn't sing, and he couldn't play guitar, which is a bit of a drawback if you're trying to be Buddy Holly!

Ron   I thought he was all right.

Yvonne   I thought that the atmosphere in the club was awful. Half of the audience weren't listening, they were just sat like they always are, presumably, waiting for the next game of bingo. And if the organist had hit the right notes once it would have been a miracle.

Ron   Oh come on, be fair . . .

Yvonne   I thought the kids who did Boyzone were backward, to be honest, and the woman who sang that song from *Titantic* was ill, you could see she was.

Ron   Yvonne be fair, they were just people who'd volunteered to get up, I mean . . .

Yvonne   Yes, but why? What was the point of it?

Ron   Well . . .

Yvonne   Utter rubbish, the whole event . . .

Ron   I don't understand you at times . . . it was all right, Grant.

Yvonne   By what criterion was it all right?

Ron   It was people just having a go at something.

Yvonne   Marks for effort rather than ability. Dumbing down.

Ron   Not necessarily . . .

Grant   Shut up a minute, you!

Ron   It was all right, Steph . . .

Grant   No, she's right, I thought it was shit, to be honest. Wasn't it, Steph . . . ?

Steph   I thought it was all right . . .

Ron   I thought it was . . .

Grant   Usually there's one or two good singers but it was awful this weekend . . .

Steph *is childishly hurt. She is becoming petulant.*

Steph   I thought Boyzone were good. I mean, they haven't had any training or owt, have they? It's not as if they're professionals or owt. It was just sommat to do. I don't know why you've had to rip 'em all to bits?

Yvonne   Well the Grunt asked me my opinion, and now nobody likes it.

Ron   Yvonne . . . !

Yvonne   I can't do what you do, I can't pretend things are better than they are, you should know that!

Grant *goes to grab* **Steph**. *She doesn't like it.*

Grant   Steph, come and sit down, you're bugging me to bloody death standing up there, you're like a fuckin' lost woman.

Steph   I'm all right!

A vicious temper.

Grant   I said come and sit down and have a fuckin' drink or sommat.

Yvonne   I thought Steph was all right actually.

Ron   I thought she did really well . . .

Yvonne   Honestly!

Steph   I thought you said it was awful?

Yvonne I thought you were quite good . . . good range, not bad at all . . .

Grant She was fuckin' rubbish, she missed half the bloody words.

Ron I thought you were great, really good.

Grant Don't patronise her, man, she was shite and she knows she was.

A beat.

Ron Well, I thought you were good.

Grant She's usually a lot better than that rubbish.

Yvonne It is nerve-wracking . . .

Steph *is very brittle.*

Steph I got nervous. Put me off. It's wi' him being a teacher. I've never liked teachers, they're always judging you!

Ron No I wasn't, I thought you were great!

A beat.

Grant So what did they finish you for then, Ron?

Ron Oh dear . . .

Grant I got finished at pit after t' strike. Thirteen thousand, what a fucking joke eh? Not even get me a caravan like yours.

Ron My nerves.

Grant They can finish you for that, can they?

Ron Well they did me. I needed to get out.

Grant Thirteen thousand!

Ron I spent every day sorting out problems.

Grant Pressure job you see . . .

Ron   I never went in a classroom.

Grant   Bit of a drawback for a teacher then!

Ron   Bloody staff having breakdowns, kids having breakdowns, pregnancies, bloody hell, you name it!

Grant   Sounds like the school I went to . . . I was a bastard at school, Yvonne, I've calmed down now a bit!

Ron   Then we had an inspection. That was fun!

Grant   Always felt they were looking down on me at school, you know?

Ron   Most of the kids were from broken homes . . .

Grant   Better off now though, eh?

Ron   We were bottom of the league table!

Grant   No more of that now, Ron.

Ron   We couldn't get any parent governors!

Grant   I told her, I'm glad they finished me. I spent six years getting over the bloody strike but I was glad to get out of the pit. I never thought I'd say that but . . .

Ron   Bloody nightmare . . .

Grant   Five years in the bloody wilderness, man! Then I met Steph, didn't I? Best thing in my life!

Ron   Smashing . . .

Grant   Two years in March int it?

Steph   Two year, in March . . .

Grant   Married twice, won't I?

Steph   Aye, he's that thick he made the same mistake, twice.

Grant   Shut up, you witch! Three kids you know? Great aren't they, we bring 'em up here some weekends, don't we?

Steph He was on his own for three years, weren't you?

Grant She's brilliant with 'em she is. Wayne, my eldest, is seventeen now, you should see him and her they're like brother and sister, are you?

Steph He's a big un, int he?

Grant Oh aye, he's a big un, he'd've made your nerves bad sorting him out, Ron.

Ron *laughs. A thin veneer covers the dialogue.*

Ron We've got three you know . . .

Grant Three girls? Oh bloody hell, I couldn't handle it. Just think what they'll get up to when they're older. Just think what men'll want to do to 'em? No. I couldn't handle that.

Ron Well . . . I don't . . .

Grant If anybody touched my little girls I'd slit their throats. Men are bastards!

Ron I know.

Grant Bastards! Our Wayne is, int he?

Steph He's a big un, int he?

Grant Mind you, some women are too to think on it!

A beat.

Yvonne Why did you get divorced then?

Grant I didn't have a relationship, love. You know what I mean?

Steph It was awful, wasn't it?

Grant Awful! Killing me, wasn't she?

Steph Killing him, wasn't she?

Grant I kid you not, Ron, but everything I did for Denise was bloody wrong for her!

Ron   Really?

Grant   Everything! I couldn't put a foot right. We'd had three kids and everything I did for that bloody woman was wrong. I wish they'd've retired me from that marriage, talk about being bad with your nerves? And the other one before her, dopey Vicky, well she was as soft as a brush. Bloody lesbian or sommat I think.

Yvonne   You didn't have any kids to her then?

Grant   Are you joking, I couldn't get bloody near her . . . The day I met Steph was the best day of my life, wasn't it?

Ron   Smashing . . .

Grant   Now is everybody all right for a drink. Yvonne?

Yvonne   No, I'm taking it steady.

Grant   She dun't want a repeat performance of last night, does she?

Steph   No wonder.

Grant   Did she tell you what happened?

Ron   Oh yes!

Grant   What a carry on. You know that she got up with 'em and all!

Ron   No?

Grant   Oh aye, she's a right one is this one, she was up with 'em dancing and rubbing oil in 'em, weren't you?

Steph   Tell everybody . . .

Grant   Oh aye, she likes to get her money's worth. I tell you she's a right un when she's out. Mind you, did she tell you what she got up to?

Yvonne   Ron knows all about it.

Grant   Funny eh?

Ron   That's right.

Grant   I mean it's only a bit of fun though, isn't it? What a pair I ask you, and they're as different again, aren't they?

Ron   They are.

Grant   But she's a maniac according to Steph. I don't know how you cope with her. Did she tell you what she let them do?

Ron   No.

Yvonne   We needn't get into all the detail, need we?

Grant   I think it's hilarious me, they didn't do it to Steph, but fancy letting 'em stuff your head down their trousers and waggle their wedding tackle in her face? I mean bloody funny! She didn't do it. But Steph said Yvonne did it twice. Must have liked it, Ron.

Ron   Must have.

Grant   Bloody funny.

Ron *is ashen.*

I bet she got a bloody eyeful then, mate!

Ron   I bet she did.

Grant   Get down, have a look at that! Bloody hell, Yvonne, you make me laugh.

Yvonne (*light, laughing*)   Well you know . . .

Grant   They both went backstage. God knows what for, couldn't get enough. Set of bloody queers. I think it's funny I do. She's a funny bugger is Yvonne, she's all prim and proper but when she's had a drink . . .

Yvonne   That's me!

Grant   Come here, you . . .

Grant *grabs* **Steph** *kindly.*

She's lovely, int she, int she lovely?

Steph   Am I?

Grant   Well are we going to call that a night then, sweetheart?

Steph   Can do.

Grant   Anyway, there's plenty of ale left if you want one.

Ron   Right!

Grant   I think Yvonne should take it steady though, I don't want anybody on the site raping!

Yvonne (*trying to keep it light*)   It's her, she's a bad influence on me.

Grant   Anyway goodnight, love. I thought you were brilliant up there, we'll do sommat tomorrow if you want!

Grant *kisses* **Yvonne**. *It is a long kiss and he feels the cup of her breast.* **Ron** *watches.*

Goodnight. I've right enjoyed your company. Hey take it steady if your nerves are bad, mate, my brother-in-law's nerves were all over the shop and he ended up gassing his fuckin' sen, didn't he?

Steph   Awful!

Grant   Come on then . . .

Grant *and* **Steph** *exit to their caravan.* **Yvonne** *and* **Ron** *sit and look at each other.* **Ron** *takes a few sips on his drink.*

Yvonne   Shall we get cleared away then? Be good to get off early . . .

Silence.

What?

Ron   Thank you.

Yvonne   For what?

Ron   For what?

Yvonne   Ron . . .

Ron   For what?

Yvonne   Oh stop it!

Ron   Why didn't you tell me?

Yvonne   What difference would it have made . . .

Ron   Bloody hell . . . !

Yvonne   Ron, it's nothing.

Ron   Nothing.

Yvonne   No.

Ron   Nothing? I've got a wife who gets drunk and lets her head get stuck down the trousers of young men? What planet are you from?

Yvonne   It was all part of it.

Ron   So that makes it all right then?

Yvonne   It was just a bit of fun that went too far. All right, it went too far, that's all!

Ron   That's all, that's all!

Yvonne   Have you never done anything you feel guilty about?

Ron (*loudly*)   You don't appear to feel guilty about it!

Yvonne   Stop shouting.

Ron   You'd go out and do it again tonight, you would!

Yvonne   Stop it!

Ron   Stop it? I'll kill you in a minute, good God I will!

Yvonne   Oh go on then!

Ron   I can't trust you, can I? I saw you one night kissing Peter after the *Showboat* party and that kiss lasted nearly a bloody hour!

Yvonne   So what?

Ron   I could swing for you . . . I could!

Yvonne   Oh go on then!

Ron   You're just not bothered, are you?

Yvonne   No I'm not and I'll tell you something else, it was the best night I've had in the last three years, if you must know.

Ron   Ah ah!

Yvonne   It was.

Ron   I've heard you!

Yvonne   It was the first time I've felt any excitement.

Ron *slaps her across the face.*

Silence.

Ron   Sorry!

Yvonne   Go on, little man. Hit me again. Go on, knock my teeth out! Slap me if that's what you want to do, slap me!

Yvonne *attacks* **Ron**. **Ron** *pathetically fights back.*

Ron   Shut up! Shut up for God's sake!

Yvonne   Go on, make a complete fool of yourself . . .

Ron   No I'll leave you to do that, shall I?

Yvonne *and* **Ron** *wrestle awkwardly as* **Grant** *comes from the caravan.*

Grant   What's going on?

Ron   Nothing.

Grant   You all right?

Yvonne   Yes.

Ron   Everything's fine, go back to bed.

Grant   Has he hit you?

Ron (*shouts*)   I said go back to bed!

Grant   Wow steady, tha's not at school now! Are you all right?

Ron (*shouts*)   Go back to bed!

Grant   You shouldn't hit women, didn't tha learn that at college?

Ron   She's all right . . .

Grant   Aye, she looks it . . . Do you want to go inside with Steph while I have a word with Ron?

Ron   Have a word? Have a word, you're the bloody reason she's like this . . .

Grant   Go inside, love.

Yvonne   Leave me, I'm all right.

Ron   Leave her . . . !

Yvonne *is very emotional.*

Yvonne   I'm sorry, Ron, Jesus Christ . . . I'm sorry . . . but I felt so alive . . .

Ron   Sorry?

Yvonne   What can I say . . . ?

Ron   I ought to kill you, I did honest . . .

Grant   Hey, hey, now steady.

Ron   Steady?

Grant   Pack it in!

Ron   Or what?

Grant   You what?

Ron   Or what? Come on then! Come on . . . ! All my life I've been running from the likes of you! You're that bloody thick it's frightening . . .

Grant   Tha what?

Yvonne   Ron just leave it . . .

Ron *picks up an HP sauce bottle and uses it as a weapon against* **Grant***. He then uses it as a penis and pretends to pass wind through the next speech. It is pathetic.*

Ron   I can be crude as the rest, if that's what you're after, is it? Is it the animal you're after? Come on, let's get you sorted out . . .

Grant   Go to bed, man, go to bed, you're not worth it.

Grant *turns.*

And keep the fuckin' noise down, some of us are trying to have a bloody holiday! Good grief, some people just don't know how to fuckin' behave!

Grant *exits.* **Ron** *stands still,* **Yvonne** *is prostrate and weeps. She grabs a can of beer.*

Yvonne   Ron . . . ?

Ron   No, don't, don't ever speak to me again . . .

Ron *begins clearing away. He puts some rubbish into his waste bag. And smells the rabbit giblets.*

Yvonne   Ron . . . ?

Ron   Have you put this rabbit in here?

Yvonne   Eh?

Ron (*shouts*)   It's theirs, isn't it? You ignorant pig . . . !

Yvonne   What a bloody weekend . . . !

Ron   What have they been playing at? Animal. Grunt!
Arsehole!

A beat.

Yvonne   What a mess . . . Gooor!

Ron   I'll start to get it cleared away then. Jeeez.

Yvonne   What can I say?

Ron (*almost in tears of desperation*)   Look at that awning, that
was a sodding waste of money and all, wasn't it? A soddin'
wash out!

Yvonne *begins to help* **Ron** *put the rubbish into a bin.*

Yvonne   Ron?

Ron   Don't . . .

Yvonne   Ron . . .

Ron   Don't say a word . . .

*They both put the rubbish into bags. Music plays softly under. Silence.
Then suddenly.*

Steph   Oh, oh, oh, Grant, oh no please, Grant no not
that!

Ron   Oh we're off!

Yvonne   Ron, please listen . . .

Ron   Are you going to go in their caravan because you're
not coming in here!

Ron *continues to put rubbish into the bag. He suddenly stops and
looks at a piece of paper.*

Well look at that . . . !

Steph   Oh, Grant, oh, no, oh, oh, oh . . .

Yvonne   What is it?

Ron   The bloody instructions for the awning.

Steph Oh, oh, oh, no . . .

Ron I can't bloody believe it . . .

Ron *goes to get the awning.*

Yvonne Leave that now . . . ! For God's sake . . .

Ron I'll get it up now I've got these . . .

Yvonne Ron, it's midnight . . .

Steph Oh, oh, oh, oh!

Ron *starts to put the awning up.* **Yvonne** *sits and has a drink.*

Ron Just listen to that . . .

Yvonne Ron, leave it please . . .

Ron Just listen to 'em. Bloody animals. Just listen to that bloody noise . . .

Steph Oh, oh, oh . . . Ah!!

A beat.

Yvonne I know, isn't it wonderful?

Kool and the Gang, 'Ladies Night' swells. **Ron** *and* **Yvonne** *begin to put up their awning, they hold a piece of the awning structure which is connected in four parts by wire, it is very floppy and difficult to control. It is a struggle for them to cope with, as lights fade to blackout.*

Methuen Modern Plays

include work by

Jean Anouilh
John Arden
Margaretta D'Arcy
Peter Barnes
Sebastian Barry
Brendan Behan
Dermot Bolger
Edward Bond
Bertolt Brecht
Howard Brenton
Anthony Burgess
Simon Burke
Jim Cartwright
Caryl Churchill
Noël Coward
Lucinda Coxon
Sarah Daniels
Nick Darke
Nick Dear
Shelagh Delaney
David Edgar
David Eldridge
Dario Fo
Michael Frayn
John Godber
Paul Godfrey
David Greig
John Guare
Peter Handke
David Harrower
Jonathan Harvey
Iain Heggie
Declan Hughes
Terry Johnson
Sarah Kane
Charlotte Keatley
Barrie Keeffe
Howard Korder

Robert Lepage
Doug Lucie
Martin McDonagh
John McGrath
Terrence McNally
David Mamet
Patrick Marber
Arthur Miller
Mtwa, Ngema & Simon
Tom Murphy
Phyllis Nagy
Peter Nichols
Joseph O'Connor
Joe Orton
Louise Page
Joe Penhall
Luigi Pirandello
Stephen Poliakoff
Franca Rame
Mark Ravenhill
Philip Ridley
Reginald Rose
Willy Russell
Jean-Paul Sartre
Sam Shepard
Wole Soyinka
Shelagh Stephenson
Peter Straughan
C. P. Taylor
Theatre de Complicite
Theatre Workshop
Sue Townsend
Judy Upton
Timberlake Wertenbaker
Roy Williams
Snoo Wilson
Victoria Wood

Methuen Contemporary Dramatists
include

Peter Barnes (three volumes)
Sebastian Barry
Edward Bond (seven volumes)
Howard Brenton
  (two volumes)
Richard Cameron
Jim Cartwright
Caryl Churchill (two volumes)
Sarah Daniels (two volumes)
Nick Darke
David Edgar (three volumes)
Ben Elton
Dario Fo (two volumes)
Michael Frayn (three volumes)
John Godber
Paul Godfrey
David Greig
John Guare
Lee Hall
Peter Handke
Jonathan Harvey
Iain Heggie
Declan Hughes
Terry Johnson (two volumes)
Sarah Kane
Bernard-Marie Koltès
David Lan
Bryony Lavery
Doug Lucie
David Mamet (four volumes)

Martin McDonagh
Duncan McLean
Anthony Minghella
  (two volumes)
Tom Murphy (four volumes)
Phyllis Nagy
Anthony Neisen
Philip Osment
Louise Page
Stewart Parker
Joe Penhall
Stephen Poliakoff
  (three volumes)
David Rabe
Mark Ravenhill
Christina Reid
Philip Ridley
Willy Russell
Ntozake Shange
Eric Emanuel Schmitt
Sam Shepard (two volumes)
Wole Soyinka (two volumes)
Shelagh Stephenson
David Storey (three volumes)
Sue Townsend
Michel Vinaver (two volumes)
Michael Wilcox
Roy William
David Wood (two volumes)
Victoria Wood

Methuen Student Editions

Jean Anouilh	*Antigone*
John Arden	*Serjeant Musgrave's Dance*
Alan Ayckbourn	*Confusions*
Aphra Behn	*The Rover*
Edward Bond	*Lear*
Bertolt Brecht	*The Caucasian Chalk Circle*
	Life of Galileo
	Mother Courage and her Children
Anton Chekhov	*The Cherry Orchard*
	The Seagull
Caryl Churchill	*Serious Money*
	Top Girls
Shelagh Delaney	*A Taste of Honey*
John Galsworthy	*Strife*
Robert Holman	*Across Oka*
Henrik Ibsen	*A Doll's House*
	Hedda Gabler
Charlotte Keatley	*My Mother Said I Never Should*
Bernard Kops	*Dreams of Anne Frank*
Federico García Lorca	*Blood Wedding*
	(bilingual edition)
John Marston	*The Malcontent*
Willy Russell	*Blood Brothers*
Wole Soyinka	*Death and the King's Horseman*
August Strindberg	*The Father*
J. M. Synge	*The Playboy of the Western World*
Oscar Wilde	*The Importance of Being Earnest*
Tennessee Williams	*A Streetcar Named Desire*
	The Glass Menagerie
Timberlake Wertenbaker	*Our Country's Good*

Methuen World Classics
include

Jean Anouilh (two volumes)
John Arden (two volumes)
Arden & D'Arcy
Brendan Behan
Aphra Behn
Bertolt Brecht (eight volumes)
Büchner
Bulgakov
Calderón
Čapek
Anton Chekhov
Noël Coward (eight volumes)
Feydean
Eduardo De Filippo
Max Frisch
John Galsworthy
Gogol
Gorky
Harley Granville Barker
    (two volumes)
Henrik Ibsen (six volumes)

Lorca (three volumes)
Marivaux
Mustapha Matura
David Mercer (two volumes)
Arthur Miller (five volumes)
Molière
Musset
Peter Nichols (two volumes)
Joe Orton
A. W. Pinero
Luigi Pirandello
Terence Rattigan
    (two volumes)
W. Somerset Maughan
    (two volumes)
August Strindberg
    (three volumes)
J. M. Synge
Ramón del Valle-Inclán
Frank Wedekind
Oscar Wilde

For a complete catalogue of Methuen Drama titles
write to:

Methuen Drama
215 Vauxhall Bridge Road
London SW1V 1EJ

or you can visit our website at:

www.methuen.co.uk

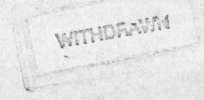